I ONCE KILLED A MAN, BUT DON'T TELL YOUR MOTHER

A Collection of Stories and Family Secrets

Darien Ogburn

NEWMAN SPRINGS PUBLISHING
320 Broad Street
Red Bank, NJ 07701

First originally published by Newman Springs Publishing 2024

ISBN 979-8-89308-576-1 (Paperback)
ISBN 979-8-89308-577-8 (Digital)

Printed in the United States of America

To my father, someone I took for granted way too often and now miss more than I would have ever imagined. Thank you, Dad, for all the wisdom, humor, love, guidance, and patience you provided to me—even when it was accidental and/or not deserved.

CONTENTS

It was cold outside. Early January weather in Georgia can be unpredictable. The cloudless sky allowed ample sunshine to lumber into the bedroom where my father lay shortly before his death. The sunlight entering the windows of his bedroom, along with the steady stream of visitors, provided a rich warmth to the small space in which Dad would spend his waning moments. Dad loved being outdoors, but the temperature and his frailty had finally put this out of reach. I clearly remember the weather that day, as I told my father the day, date, and weather when I came into the room. I've heard from others that people on their deathbeds want to know the date they are expected to die, so I thought it would be something Dad would want to know as well. I don't know if he heard me, but I still whispered into his ear, "It's Friday, January 6, 2012, and it is damn cold outside." That was the last time I talked to him (not the last thing I said, though), as he passed away the next day. Second only to the day my son died, this was the most difficult time in my life.

I recount the story above to explain why I've come to feel the need to write this book. About a week before Dad died, I was at the house my father shared with my mother for the preceding twenty years. I, along with my sister Michele, our mother, my wife Tracey, and a few others time has erased from my memory were there to stand vigil as my father approached his last few days on earth. While we were in the living room bantering about something innocuous, I heard the groans and shuffling of Dad being assisted by the hospice nurse down the short hall from his room to join us. No doubt he needed help at this point, something he had spurned for many years. It's hard seeing your father progress in life to a point that he is so different from all your memories—a strong, confident, able-bodied, often jovial, and engaged man reduced to his final self: weak, emotionally flat, struggling to expel words between his labored breaths. I have so many memories of Dad being very physically engaged in typical human pursuits: coaching my Little League baseball teams, playing in the annual coaches' softball game, working on cars, cutting grass—so many things that are never to happen again. I, like so many others in similar circumstances, struggled to witness this play, even now so many years later.

It was obvious he was in pain as he situated himself in a chair in the small living room he'd known intimately for the last two decades. After saying a few things about his love for us all, he continued, "Ask me anything you'd like to know. I won't be here much longer, and I want you to have all the answers you need." Taken aback by the question, a million things came to mind, most of which I didn't feel entitled to know. After all, I'm just his son, not his spouse, mother, or pastor. The point here is his question has permeated my brain for the last decade. After some pretty emotional introspection, I've come to realize that Dad's unspoken memories died the day he slipped into the next part of his human journey.

Despite all the opportunities I had to talk with Dad in the days leading up to his death, I only asked him one question. My final question was of no real consequence, but it kept me close to him (both his physical presence and the presence of his voice) a few minutes longer. He was able to lucidly answer without falling into a non-verbal period or rambling into an incoherent soliloquy, as we had seen over the course of the last few days of his life. His offer for us to ask him anything could have driven me to ask him more about his upbringing or who he would place on his list of heroes. What about his first marriage? What was the motivation in moving his young family from his birthplace across the country to California? What were the circumstances that stirred him to pack everything back up in that same Buick and return to Georgia just a year later? What are some of his fondest memories of me? So many things I wish I had engaged him in well before his final days, but this was my last chance, and I couldn't polish my inquiries into something that had a chance to significantly improve my experience. Instead, I asked him where he was stationed when he was in the Navy. I suspect this popped into my mind because just prior to me asking him this question, Dad explained that the dress shoes I was wearing looked like GI boots… they didn't. Dad's awareness was definitely fading, but his memory was still present enough to let me know he spent his Navy days at the United States Naval Training Center in Bainbridge, Maryland. In all the time I spent with Dad, I never knew this little facet of his life. As insignificant as it is, I'm glad I asked him the question. As time continues to pass for me, I wish more now than ever that I had more time to ask him more *insignificant* questions.

While I didn't need to know all the things he encountered in his life, I understand the desire for my father to have his experiences live on beyond his time here on earth. These experiences, really just the recounting of them, offer the soliloquist a chance to absolve themselves of some of the wrongs they've committed in their life, or they can also be a gift to recipients in the form of words of wisdom, acceptance, forgiveness, or enlightenment so much needed for those being left behind. There's something alluring about having your stories somehow immortalized. In fact, there's even a named phobia related to this: athazagoraphobia—the fear of forgetting or being forgotten. Before humans crafted written language, verbal accounts and the occasional cave drawing were all there was to keep someone's experiences alive. Not only can you learn from the experiences of others, you can also be entertained, shocked, humbled, and awed by how varied and full a life they've lived.

There's no doubt many of my father's memories died with him that day, but I'm not here to try and piece together his experiences. Those were his stories, and while I wish I would have asked him more questions when he was alive, I am content to only share some of his wisdom and wit here, as it is now part of my own experience. The bottom line here is I do not want my memories to die with me—well, maybe some of them. I have recited many of the following anecdotes so many times that my children are beginning to think they lived them themselves. Other recollections are a bit more obscure and rarely, if ever, mentioned by me or anyone else seemingly in the know. I'm sure some of the things mentioned will be cringe-worthy to some (or many), but most will be recollections of experiences I do not want to die when I too slip into the next phase of my voyage.

In preparation for this book, I consumed many memoirs looking for inspiration beyond my father's solicitation. I've recognized writing styles and story content similar to mine, but there is one blinding difference between my station in life and those of the authors I studied: the subjects of all the memoirs I read had some degree of popular notoriety. I have a couple of *claims to fame*, but nothing approaching the renown or celebrity of television or movie stars, comedians, politicians, professional athletes, or artists. So I understand the higher the name recognition, the more likely people are to buy (and more importantly consume/experience) a memoir. But the measure of success in this endeavor, at least my yardstick, is that those closest to me have a chance to reminisce along with me as I recount some of the things I find interesting about my own human experience.

When he learned about my intentions to write this book, a very close friend said that after reading autobiographies and biographies he "sometimes wondered why the person bothered to write about themselves because their life wasn't all that fascinating." I didn't receive his comments as an indictment of my experiences or intent to memorialize them, but more as his reaction to someone's insistence that he himself write an autobiography, as he didn't consider his life to be extraordinary or all that interesting. From the inside looking out, I can see why he might think his life isn't worth immortalizing on paper. I have the same general feeling about my own life. However, looking from the outside in, I've only had a fractional picture of some of the incredibly interesting tidbits of his history, and I'd love to learn more about those morsels. My children often ask me about certain parts of my history, and I even have the good fortune to have nonfamily members ask me about certain parts of my past. I like to think that I've found a way to recount many of these stories in ways that don't waste the questioner's time with a simple (and boring) response. Occasionally, I embellish the facts, but I never cross the line into overt fiction, although you may question this claim in a few of the following anecdotes. Despite the inner voice encouraging me to take my stories to the grave, I've decided to document some of my experiences here with the hope you find some nuggets of interest and/or value, thereby prolonging my existence here on earth.

A number of years ago, I recall a television journalist who would throw a dart at a map of the United States to determine where he'd go to interview some unknown person. After arriving in the town, he'd then go to a phone booth in the middle of town and randomly select a name from the local phone book. I know there were likely some shenanigans going on with exactly how this feature was produced, as presumably some people would likely have no interest in being filmed or interviewed. Nonetheless, it came off as if this reporter was able to ferret out some incredible stories from unheralded folks who lived quiet and unassuming lives—like living their entire adult life without having told anyone (including their spouse) that they had received the Medal of Honor for heroics in the Korean War, or living a modest life while donating most of their earnings to anonymously provide scholarships to local children so they could get an education the benefactor never obtained. There were some shocking revelations as well, but the spectacle of it all is less intriguing to me than the incredible stories of how some human beings got way more out of life than you could ever have imagined by just looking at them. Basically, everyone has a story to tell—all you have to do is be curious, ask questions, and mostly listen. Obscurity allows many incredibly fascinating experiences to be lost in the crevices of time. Now I'm not saying my life has been *incredibly fascinating*, but I think you might find some of the following anecdotes mildly humorous, and maybe even be encouraged to memorialize some of your own for others to enjoy.

According to the US Centers for Disease Control and Prevention, the average life expectancy in 2020 for residents of the United States is 77.8 years. That equates to approximately 40,919,688 minutes the average person has to experience life. So far, I've used up about thirty million of my minutes. While I was never awarded a Medal of Honor and have never sponsored a scholarship for anyone, like everyone else, I've had some experiences in my life that I'd like to see live on, if only with my family members. It's impossible not to have something to reflect on after having spent this much time on earth.

There is another voice I battle with as I write this book: It continuously reminds me there are too many people out there opining about one issue or another. They do this with such ease, eloquence, and confidence that others seem to accept their message as gospel because they have a visible platform from which to espouse their beliefs. Therefore, I will try my best to avoid making statements of value (or politic) so as not to take advantage of my millions of dedicated followers. Hopefully, by the end of this book, you'll recognize the sarcasm in my comments (like that in the last sentence).

If you actually purchased this book, thank you. In fact, since this is effectively intended for an audience of three, I anticipate I either gave you this book or I have already sent you a personalized thank-you note for buying it! In addition to venerating some good memories that have been woven into my experience, I've also decided that now is the time to acknowledge to a larger audience one of the darker parts of my existence. The book title points to something all of my immediate family already knows, and for very good reason, deliberately chooses not to discuss.

I suppose there are a number of ways a person can find themselves in a situation where killing another human being might seem like a completely rational decision. Crimes of passion (e.g., lover's quarrel, road rage, being personally maligned, etc.) are, by definition, irrational responses to commonly experienced circumstances. However, there are instances where someone feels they have been aggrieved to such an extent that they go to extraordinary effort to contemplate and plan complex capital retribution. From a legal standpoint, the length of time one envisages exacting revenge assigns the intent of *premeditation* and removes the moniker of a *heat of passion* action, changing the charge from manslaughter to murder.

I suspect many others have experienced similar situations to mine in their lives but have not given serious consideration to taking another person's life. My specific history, whether tied to my genetic makeup or to environmental experiences, has actually contributed to my deep involvement in planning the death of another person. I'm not proud of this pronouncement, but it is the simple recognition of one of my many flaws. This book will weave you through some of my experiences to give you a preview of how my story was written and where I am after many years of reflection.

Oh, and by the way, for my children and wife…I am not dying (that I know of). So this is an example of one of the few times I did something before the deadline.

A special thanks goes to my wife Tracey and our two children, Savana and Nicholas. Their continuous encouragement for me to write this book has resulted in just that. Although I suspect they wanted me to write all of these things down on paper so they don't have to continually endure countless verbal recollections of these same stories. Thanks, family...I think.

And to Jon-Michael, you taught me more in seven hours and one minute than I've learned in my other thirty million minutes so far.

In the Beginning...

Wednesday, December 23, 1964. That's it...all I remember.

Building Blocks

Why do I react to things differently than others? Why do I have an affinity for vanilla ice cream? Where in the world did I get this scar? Like many people, I have a million questions about my current state and what history contributed to who I am today. I've wondered these things for many years, and it wasn't until I began researching this book and memorializing my past that I began to make some connections. The mathematician and meteorologist Edward Norton Lorenz posited that the details of a tornado (e.g., when it forms, the path it takes, etc.) could be significantly influenced by minor agitations (say the distant flapping of a butterfly's wings several weeks earlier). I'm not sure if a butterfly lifting off from a Shasta daisy in Japan in the waning weeks of 1964 has anything to do with my love for baseball, but I believe there are some contributors to my construction that are a little more connected to me than Lorenz's Butterfly Theory. Some events in my life, no matter how insignificant they may seem, I postulate can be tied back to who I am today. Both causation and correlation be damned, the only rule to which my hypothesis can be positively tied is the rule of temporal precedence.

There are several events early in my life that assuredly helped build my personality. For every story I recount below, there are probably five or ten more I could use. So you're welcome in advance for the relative brevity of this particular chapter.

Humor

Over the years, I've explained to whomever would listen that I was born in the next-to-last week of the last month of the last year of the baby boom generation. As far as I can tell, this has absolutely no bearing on anything in my life. I suspect some well-heeled sociologist would be able to piece together some connection between my experiences and the generation to which I am assigned. But I'm not convinced being at the very end of an eighteen-year epoch allows me any truly common experience with someone at the beginning (or middle) of the same semi-arbitrary time frame. For example, I have a faint recollection of the war in Vietnam, whereas that entire episode of the American experience was received in a much different light by someone even slightly more senior to me. After all, America officially sent troops into Vietnam just prior to my birth, and I was just ten years old when the US unceremoniously retreated. So I wasn't directly involved in the conflict, and the larger portion of my assigned *generation* was being drafted and moving through time with a completely different perspective and experience.

The nightly news was not of interest to me when I was young, so my exposure to the war was only what I experienced through my family. I remember vividly the worry my parents had for many of the young men in our extended family and what their fate would be if they were drafted into the armed forces. My cousin Louie was one of those who found himself in precisely that situation. My memories of how all of this unfolded are very foggy, but family reunion conversations and some old *Super 8* movies have helped supplement some of the feelings I do recall. There was a specific family get-together intended to serve as a joint going-away party for Louie as he prepared to ship off to Vietnam and a birthday party for my mother. The smell of candles, cigarettes, sweet cake icing, and pork chops on the grill still permeate my memory of this *celebration*. Smell is the most primitive of the senses, and therefore the one most likely to generate long-term associations without distortions. This is because smell signals go directly from receptors in the nose to the olfactory bulb, bypassing the thalamus. Some may say that going back to their childhood home (or school, or other location from their youth) or hearing a song from a particularly important time in their life generates strong associative memories. There is no doubt this is true, but vision and hearing are processed through the thalamus, degrading the associations by allowing new information and perspectives to attach to the experience. Have you ever gone back to your elementary school and said to yourself, "Wow, it's much smaller than I remember"? But the smell of freshly sharpened pencils and dusty erasers takes you to how you felt at a specific moment in third grade. So, any time I smell birthday cake candles, cigarettes, pork chops on the grill, or very sweet cake icing (separately or together), I immediately return to the birthday/going-away party that happened more than fifty years ago.

Watching old *Super 8* films of this get-together has helped me understand something that is a big part of who I am. Specifically, while everyone came together to spend time with Louie before he went off to war, there was a palpable sense of worry that he wouldn't come back alive. However, the film shows everyone laughing and cutting up in a way that masked any stress with the circumstance. I can still see Aunt Jimmie (Louie's mother) sitting at the kitchen table, smoking a cigarette, and hearing her sharp cackle as jokes were thrown about that day. She did this with her eyes wide open, knowing her eldest son was about to go off to a war in a faraway land. Looking back and putting this into perspective instructs how I tend to deal with challenging situations—almost to a fault. It is clear that my family (my entire extended family, in fact) obscures their fear with laughter and joy. I'm sure they handle things differently in small and more intimate settings, but they use laughter as a way to trudge through very difficult times when we come together as a larger group.

As mentioned above, I don't think this is tied to being part of the baby boom generation, but more as an Ogburn way of dealing with difficult things. So I think my family has taught me to approach difficult situations with humor. You'll see this approach plaited throughout many of my experiences. Sometimes the humor comes well after the experience, but it will inevitably manifest itself.

By the way, Louie did come back from Vietnam alive, and we were fortunate to have him with us for another twenty years.

Pain Tolerance

What's the earliest memory you have as a child? Most people I've asked come up with something around four or five years old. Maybe it was a birthday party or their grandmother's handmade fried apple pies or something else generally positive. For me, the first memory I have was as a toddler at about three years old—it was a traumatic experience that cannot at all be considered an implanted memory. I say this because I mentioned this incident to my mother a few years back, and she only had a fleeting recollection of the event. There were never any funny anecdotes passed along during family get-togethers to introduce the memory to me. So the fact I was the one that brought this to my mother so many years later tells me it is more than likely a real memory.

Nonetheless, I was about three years old when my family was preparing to move from one house to another. My parents rented a moving truck to transfer all our belongings to the new house. After the truck was loaded and it came time to close the roller door, my finger happened to be in the exact spot for the door to pinch it when it rolled down on its track. Being more than fifty years ago, I don't recall the extent of the pain, but my reaction must have indicated a sufficient amount to cause my mother to calm me down by giving me ice cream. Not a terribly exciting story, like say being dragged out of camp by a jackal and being raised by its extended pack for the next three years, but one that might explain why I tend to be a big baby when it comes to pain even today. And I've learned the added bonus that if you cry loudly enough, someone will likely give you ice cream.

Performer

It's hard to say, but sometime around the same time as the ice cream event mentioned above (carbon dated to about 1968), I was playing in the yard with my brother and sisters outside our house beneath the tall pines and amidst the scraggly hedges that formed the border of our yard. Perhaps the situation isn't fully seated in my brain to allow for a Technicolor-versioned memory, but I recall our yard being very shaded, wanting of grass, and therefore devoid of color beyond the brownish-red hue of the Georgia clay-clad yard. The lack of grass is what offered the ingredients for what was to come.

At some point in the day, my sister Chris, thinking I wouldn't be so guileless to accept, offered me a freshly made mud pie. I thought it would be funny to eat one and see her reaction. Well, much to Chris's astonishment, I accepted her savory, organic culinary concoction and proceeded to take a few bites. When she witnessed this, she ran wide-eyed inside to tell our mother of my transgression. Chris's reaction was exactly what I was looking for, and our mother's response was the icing on the cake. Mom's declaration that I would get worms from eating dirt punctuated the fact that this would be the subject of family conversation for the next several days. I garnered so much attention by expending so little effort. I don't think I got worms, as I suspect that would have changed this from an attention-getting celebration to a traumatic memory (and perhaps a bowl of ice cream would have followed). I still get a kick out of doing something surprising just to see how others react.

Negotiator

My brother Robby and I are separated by just fifteen months, with Robby being the eldest. Growing up, we had to do just about everything together. We shared the same bedroom, bathed together, and were even relegated to using the restroom together. You see, we lived in a small house with just one bathroom for two adults and four children at the time (my younger sister Deanne had yet to arrive). We were also required to share toys, and sometimes it wasn't clear which toys *belonged* to me and which to Robby.

One day, Robby had taken control of the metal Tonka fire truck just before we were told to take advantage of the open bathroom. Thinking I had some leverage here to get the fire truck back, I demanded Robby give it to me. His refusal resulted in my delivery of an ultimatum: "Give me the fire truck, or I'll pee on you!" Again, he refused. So being a *man of my word*, I provided him with said retribution. Funny, all these years later, I don't remember if I ever saw that fire truck again, or even if I got punished for keeping true to my promise, although I suspect Mom and Dad laughed harder about this than I cried.

Ironically, Robby went on to a career as a firefighter, and I absolutely abhor negotiating anything now. Perhaps I'm afraid that if I'm not successful, karma will return the favor and someone will urinate on me.

Outsider/Loner

My mother has told me that as a child, I was content to play alone in my playpen all day long. I still enjoy being alone, although I would rather do so out of the playpen nowadays. I don't recall having many birthday parties growing up. In fact, I think I was probably about seven or eight when I had my first one that included friends (not just my parents and siblings). I was pretty uncomfortable in group settings, particularly when I was supposed to be the center of attention.

I remember having a number of friends over for my birthday party this particular year and not feeling terribly interested in spending time with anyone. At one point, everyone decided to get together outside and play football—this was well before the overly structured and programmed birthday "events" of today. I decided I was content to let them have their fun while I played with my *Emergency!* action figures. For those of you who don't know, *Emergency!* was a TV series in the early to mid-1970s about the Los Angeles County

Fire Department's Paramedical Rescue Service. I had a couple of *Emergency!* action figures (Paramedics Gage and Roy) that I decided would be better company than all the real people gathered in the front yard playing a game of football. I remember wondering if they thought I was some sort of freak or something for not joining the football game. But that thought was fleeting because I realized Gage and Roy needed to attend to my Evel Knievel action figure, who had just had a terrible accident trying to jump over an RV on his motorcycle.

I'm not exactly sure when this all took a turn to conspiracy, but I had a theory on why I didn't fit in with others when I was growing up. This is something I have never divulged to my family, so this will likely come as a shock to them. It was clear, at least to me, that I was different from my contemporaries. I tended to think deeply (yes, overthink) about things and was usually confounded by people who reacted to things without much reflection. So I determined I was actually the only human being in my family, and everyone else was an extraterrestrial inserted into my life to learn how real humans react to things in natural settings. Who knew extraterrestrials had such serious scientific skill and rigor?

When something happened that I didn't understand, I decided not to react to it so as not to give the aliens the satisfaction of learning how earthlings responded to different stimuli. There was no way I was going to give in to this intrusion of our planet. So I decided I should probably stick to being alone most of the time and avoid telling anyone what I was thinking or feeling. Thinking back on this now, though, I suspect this has contributed to some type of psychosis that prevents me from building deep relationships with others (both humans and aliens). This is something I'm sure our otherworldly observers would want to better understand, so I think I'll keep this all to myself.

CHAPTER 3

A Little About Me

Immediate family

Three siblings (two sisters and one brother) preceded me in my immediate family. The firstborn was Michele Elaine (Michele), who arrived about eleven months after Mom and Dad were married. Christa Leigh (Chris) followed about two years later, while Robert Michael (Robby) was introduced to the family another year after that. Fifteen months later, I was born to even out the gender competition in our brood. Seven years after I was born, the male/female ratio was finally decided when Mom and Dad brought Bebe Deanne (Deanne) home to give the girls a slight advantage in the X-Y chromosomal chase.

I've heard from Mom many times that people used to look at me when I was an infant and exclaim, "That baby is too pretty to be a boy." Now I'm not sure what that means, but I suspect it was a generic compliment about any newborn of the time—sort of like saying, "Oh, your baby is just adorable." Nonetheless, it's a message that has been replayed in our family for many years and has attached to me like super glue. You see, all of my siblings believe I am our mother's favored child. Understanding the object of such affection is likely to be unaware of its presence. I find it difficult to fathom I have some sort of comportment to my mother's favor over that of her other children. Using a debate club tactic, I've tried to deconstruct the argument of my opponent by attempting to build a case from their point of view:

- I was the baby of the family for seven years. This is true, but you would think if being the baby of the family was the principal factor, Mom's affection would have shifted to Deanne in 1972.

- I was the first of the children to graduate from college. Another true statement, but one that needs to be qualified with the fact that both Robby and Michele have far exceeded my academic endeavors with their master's and nursing degrees, respectively. I advance that academic success should generally be celebrated by the level you achieve and not necessarily by the expediency of said accomplishment.

- I lived at home longer than everyone else. Once again, this is true. I counter this by saying that my experience living at home in my late teens and early twenties was not because Mom made it easier for me but because I was more accomplished in deflecting or avoiding the direct wrath she offered to everyone living under her roof. I also had so many things to do (i.e., attend college, study, work after classes and on the weekends) that I was rarely around the house to withstand Mom's constant directed pressures for me to leave. That's not to say I didn't feel indirect pressure to vacate her home—I did. Mom is accomplished at passive-aggressive criticism, and I was (and continue to be) as ripe a target as anyone else. I just did not have the means to leave the house, so I stayed until I got married.

- Mom dotes on me and my accomplishments more than she does the other children. Mom may be a proud mother when recounting my successes, but I have witnessed her pride in the other children as well. She is quick to say that Michele is an incredibly giving person and a hard worker, and her pride shines brightly when she mentions Michele's late-in-life career change to become a nurse. Mom is also equally prideful when she talks about Robby's success in his career and education. I just think they are rarely around whenever she does this, though.

Now that I think about it, these counterpoints sound more like defensiveness than explanation. No matter what challenges we have with our mother, I think the argument can easily be settled with the fact that now Mom doesn't readily answer my phone calls or return them the way she seems to when Michele or Robby reaches out to her. Maybe that's the jealous reaction of the favored child when he doesn't get the attention he's so used to receiving from his mother. It could also be that my siblings are all part of the extraterrestrial experiment, introducing this stimulus into the environment to see how I'll react. Dang it. I think I'll change my answer to "I don't care" and see if that throws the principal investigator's hypothesis into disarray.

Characteristic Traits

OCD

I'm a counter. I count everything…many times over. For example, I know there are sixteen steps to the bonus room in our house that our daughter Savana used to claim as her bedroom. Specifically, there are eight steps to the landing and eight additional steps to the bonus room. The same stair pattern meets me each time I visit the basement of our house: eight steps, a landing, and then eight final steps that allow me to descend into my favorite part of the house. We've lived in this dwelling for more than twenty years, but I still count the stairs each time I descend or ascend them. Incidentally, the count has never changed despite how many times I make the voyage.

I don't consider this a hobby, or even something that could be contrived as a *safety habit* so I could find my way up or down the stairs in the event of a power failure or if smoke fills the stairwell. Rather, this is one of the many quirks attached to my experience that seems to offer me no real benefit at all. However, for some reason, I am comforted by this ritual while others react on a gradient of amused to aggravated. Most folks that don't know me well find this to be a strange and entertaining caveat about me. I think my wife finds this characteristic to be trifling and an impediment to using quiet time for deeper thought or conversation with those who accompany me on these journeys.

When Savana was about ten, Tracey and I took her on vacation to Paris. Nicholas didn't accompany us on this trip, as this was during his "I'm afraid to fly" phase. Nevertheless, Savana, Tracey, and I were visiting the Arc de Triomphe and decided to use the roof of the monument as a vantage point to photograph the City of Light with the Carolina blue and cloudless sky as a backdrop. Being me, I was in the midst of counting the steps on our way up when others, obviously in better shape than I, raced past and caused me to miscount at about the halfway point. Up to this point, Savana and Tracey had been talking while I was resolutely quiet (I was counting, after all). I was perceptibly angry by this slight and Savana, realizing I was likely more interested in counting than engaging in time-passing conversation, immediately stopped talking and didn't rev back up until we reached the summit.

While my ascending count was suspect, I was able to get a firm count of 287 steps on the way down to street level. Nowadays, you can go online and learn trivia like this without having to actually put in the work to get the answer. I just checked and found Google incorrectly puts the count at 284. So this is evidence that not everything you read on the Internet is true!

I was explaining this element of my being to a work colleague a few years ago and I offered a couple of examples for her to witness the soundness of my commitment. I explained the stairs in the building we were in had a pattern of thirteen steps on the outside staircase and twelve on the reverse set of stairs. I went on to proudly declare the parking deck from the second level to the street was patterned with landings separated by eight steps, nine steps, seven steps, seven steps, seven steps, and a final flight of seven steps. Her response, not at all the enthusiastic amazement and reverence for which I was expecting, was to remind me the *D* in OCD stands for *disorder*.

In addition to counting, I also have a propensity to have things in order. I like the soup cans in the pantry to face outward, and I am comforted by having all the tools in my toolbox separated into categories and placed in labeled drawers. Furthermore, I assign the individual tools in order of size inside each drawer. Over the years of living with others who don't share my mania, I have lost interest in keeping the cereal boxes in alphabetical order—although this would make it much easier to grab the box of Count Chocula instead of Raisin Bran early in the morning when the lighting is low. I do get a bit touchy when things aren't where I expect them to be (re: my tools), but I've begun to mellow with age. Besides, I have accumulated a good number of duplicate tools over the years and I can usually replace a missing screwdriver that someone (Savana) has borrowed and not returned to its assigned home.

This characteristic lends itself to my ability to break down projects into small efforts to meet some larger objective—like how one might approach planning something for which they hope to accomplish without being identified and held accountable.

Punctuality

I would rather be one hour early than one minute late. Like most of my oddities, the genesis of this trait isn't clear to me, at least not as I began writing this book. In fact, spending the better part of a year steadily pounding keys (mostly the backspace and delete keys) has been both cathartic and enlightening for me.

I get incredibly uptight when I have to wait to get started on any sort of journey. Whether it's to go to work, a sporting event, or the airport or train station for a vacation, I absolutely despise the uncertainty that I will make it on time. So I tend to push everyone accompanying me to get out the door way earlier than is needed or even practical. The common recommendation is to arrive at the airport two hours before your flight, so I like to be out of the house three and a half hours before the flight. This timetable allows ample time for unexpected traffic. Most rational people will say (and have told me many times) that the two-hour buffer at the airport is enough to account for unexpected traffic. I usually listen politely and then proceed with my plan to make everyone deal with my anxieties by sitting at the airport gate for about two hours every time.

Nicholas and I had season tickets for the Atlanta Braves a few years back. I didn't miss the first pitch of any of the thirty-six games I attended that year. In fact, I was usually one of the first couple dozen people at the gates each game. This means that anyone accompanying me to the game (Nicholas went to about eighteen games with me that year) had to sit in our seats and watch the ground crew prepare the field while we ate our meal before the teams went into the locker rooms to dress for the game. I suspect I was arriving at the stadium before some of the players themselves arrived. That's just fine with me, as I didn't have to stress about traffic, parking, lines for food, or sharing the entire section with anyone except my seatmate while I ate my dinner.

What also caused me stress was knowing I couldn't avoid the crowds or traffic when I left the game. So I found myself beginning to dread going to the games altogether. While I could somewhat control the arrival stresses, I couldn't standardize my departure routine to avoid the crowds and traffic.

During the COVID-19 pandemic of 2019 to 2022, I found myself relishing staying inside. This wasn't because I was fearful of getting sick while out and about, but because staying in was so much less burdensome. I didn't have to deal with traffic, crowds, lines, waiting at restaurants, etc. Looking back on this now, I believe I was approaching an agoraphobic diagnosis. I've learned to regulate this predilection by trying to see value in unanticipated experiences. I've heard people say that getting lost on vacation was one of the best things that could've happened, as they found something they never would have dreamed of had they stayed on the anticipated path. I've experienced that myself a time or two, so I try to tell myself that detours are opportunities and not dead ends or complete wastes of time. And the first step in this journey is to actually leave your abode. Another thing that has assisted in my struggle here is that the GPS app Waze is pretty darn accurate at estimating my arrival times.

Noises

Another trait that many in my family are well aware of is my struggle with misophonia. According to Google, *misophonia* is "a disorder in which certain sounds trigger emotional or physiological responses that some might perceive as unreasonable given the circumstance." Sounds like dripping water, snapping gum, and repetitive noises, such as pencil tapping and cricket chirping, drive me crazy. Google continues with, "People with misophonia can become irritated, enraged, or even panicked when they hear their trigger sounds." I absolutely abhor the sound of someone chewing with their mouth open (smacking), snoring (even though I'm told I am afflicted with this condition myself), gulping or slurping, groaning, or anything somewhat related to bodily mechanics. This is something that has affected me from the time I was a child and has only gotten more pronounced with age.

The only effective treatment for me is to extract myself from the situation or to actually make a disgusted face and shake violently enough for the offending party to recognize my aversion and change their behavior. As you might imagine, this defense option isn't well suited for establishing or maintaining healthy relationships with other human beings. So I do what I can to suppress my natural tendencies here and try to internalize my repulsion. I recognize this is my problem to solve and not the responsibility of those around me to adjust their way of living just to make me comfortable. Understanding this, however, does not reduce the anxiety that washes over me when someone gulps their drink, slurps soup, or chomps on ice. Despite the disquiet I experience in these situations, I have yet to be so repulsed that I feel the need to kill someone for eating with their mouth open.

As part of an experimental psychology class at Oglethorpe University, I was tasked with designing an experiment to test out a hypothesis related to some routine activity. At the time, I was living at home with Mom and Dad in their cedar-planked house. Not only was this house comfortable for humans (my alien family), but it was very attractive to crickets as well. Studying in the quiet afternoons when everyone else was at work (or school) was often interrupted by the clicking sounds of crickets. The arrhythmic nature of these sounds was so distracting to me that I would go to extraordinary efforts to silence the chirping of this Orthoptera order of the Insecta family. And just in case you're wondering, no, spraying WD-40 underneath the baseboards of my bedroom did nothing to deter those little bastards.

I wondered if the sounds of crickets were as distracting to others as they were to me, or if it might even be comforting white noise to others. So I devised a study that would allow me to introduce these types of noises to unassuming students attempting to do routine mathematical equations. I had three groups of participants in this study:

1.   the control group who were allowed to complete their tasks devoid of any artificial auditory stimuli beyond what is found in a solitary office;
2.   a group unknowingly doing these tasks with a faint rhythmic tapping (like a metronome); and
3.   a group unknowingly introduced to a faint arrhythmic tapping similar to my experiences with the crickets.

The short story on the results of my study is that I either didn't provide the stimuli in the experimental groups loudly enough for them to be affected, or others are not at all bothered by the same things I am. Thank goodness I received an A for this effort despite having results that were not statistically significant, as I didn't need to go any further to determine if I was flawed myself or if I just was sloppy with the volume level on the auditory supplier (tape recorder). To protect my self-esteem, I accept the latter to be more plausible in this instance.

Frugality

There were several instances in my childhood when I witnessed Mom and Dad sitting at the kitchen table discussing which bill(s) they would forgo for the month because they couldn't afford to pay for everything. I distinctly remember the points made in these discussions and now find it strange that a seven-year-old would actually know that three mortgage payments could be missed before the bank would start the foreclosure process and that the water wouldn't be cut off if you missed the payment for one month. Despite how deprived this sounds, it was a strong motivator for me. So, I'm confident it is this memory that has driven me to be semi-miserly throughout most of my adult life.

The typical symptoms of frugality are easy to identify, from using coupons to going to matinee movie showings. I continue to give strong deference to restaurant choices based on whether I have a coupon or if my AARP card provides me with a discount. I also tend to put off non-essential expenses indefinitely because I tell myself I need to wait until I can afford it…which typically means that I never get around to making the purchase. When I was in my early teens, I developed a love for the C3 Chevrolet Corvette (1968 through 1982 body styles). When I mentioned this to my cousin Louie at the time, he responded that by the time I would be able to afford a Corvette, I wouldn't want one. Louie's prediction wasn't far off from my experience. His response helped me to better understand my "purchase procrastination" tendencies. That is, I still love these Corvettes, and I can afford one now, but I still won't pull the trigger.

My experience in this arena is manifest in other actions that include the indoctrination of others in my affliction. Nicholas was about four or five when we began to notice those Coinstar machines in the local grocery stores. Stray coins could often be found on the floor around these machines. I would encourage Nicholas to survey the area around these machines every time we entered the store with the hopes he could find some free money. It wasn't long before he would prepare to accompany me to the grocery store by collecting a wooden ruler to use underneath these machines. It became a regular practice for us to make a beeline to the Coinstar machine every time we went grocery shopping. Now I don't think we collected more than a few dollars over the years, but you would have thought we were expecting to hit the motherlode the way we would mine this area of the store.

Coca-Cola had a promotion in the early 2000s where you could collect points from special codes attached to their products. You could redeem these points for discounts to local restaurants and amusement parks, but our family routinely redeemed our points to get free DVD rentals from Blockbuster. I was forever soliciting points from family and friends who didn't collect them for themselves. I also had the tendency to pick up stray bottles I found lying around. Again, Nicholas was about four or five when we took a family vacation to Walt Disney's *Animal Kingdom*. Disney sold 20-ounce Coke products that had these codes printed on the inside of the bottle caps. Interestingly, a large number of people who purchased these products discarded the points/caps in the garbage cans around the park. Nicholas and I noticed this and decided we could collect a ton of points by taking advantage of others' thoughtlessness.

After collecting several dozen caps at *Animal Kingdom* that day, I finally began to realize how silly it was beginning to look to others (especially Tracey and Savana) when I found myself hanging Nicholas upside down into a garbage can to retrieve another bottle underneath about two feet of refuse. So I pulled Nicholas out of the garbage can and took him to the nearest restroom to wash up from several hours of sticky bottle mining. We actually banked enough points from this trip to secure Blockbuster coupons well beyond when the last Blockbuster in Georgia went out of business.

Tracey and others with whom I am surrounded on a regular basis consider me to be *cheap*. I prefer to be labeled *thrifty*.

Relationships

I have very few friends. Strike that. I have very few close friends with whom I can be myself. These people are why I live—how I live. Without this small group of chosen family, I would not be alive today. I've had a couple of bumps in my life, not unlike anyone else, but if it were not for the love, support, compassion, patience, and shoulders and ears of these folks, I would have likely given up on more than a few occasions. That's not to say that my family wasn't there for me during these struggles—they were. It was the combination of support from both friends and family that sustained me during the darkest days of my life. But there is something incredibly enveloping that comes from the support you get from those not bound by blood or marriage. I'm not easy to deal with, so those who can do it seem to have some superpower that draws me even closer to them.

Again, living for fifty-plus years gives one many opportunities, in experience and in making connections with others. I have met and enjoyed the company of lots of people, most of whom I have appreciated. I consider many to be friends and designate very few as *acquaintances*. I enjoy the company of most people, but I cannot live without the company of my chosen family. Some are friendships bound in high school, which I get to indulge in on very rare occasions. The years don't seem to interfere with our bonds, as we efficiently pick up discussions that are sometimes dormant for years when we're able to slow down our lives a bit to come together from different parts of the country. Others are neighbors from long ago who shared a similar early adulthood navigating young marriages and starting families at roughly the same time. Still, others are friendships that began with a common profession in public health. Every one of these friend groups shares a single common thread: they all held us closely when Tracey and I endured the loss of our first son. Along with our immediate and extended families, Tracey, Savana, and Nicholas, these close friends are the people to whom I owe my life.

These foibles in my personality have definitely affected my life experiences, and some of the following anecdotes will give you a glimpse into why I have developed some of these physiognomies. My experiences here are not dissimilar to those of millions (or billions) of human beings, so you may recognize some familiar things and think, *Why am I reading about someone (and something) so common and mundane?* My answer is that you've already invested a few bucks in this book, so why not go ahead and finish it? You may have also been intrigued by the title and want to learn more about someone else's family secrets—especially how someone could get to the point of taking the life of another human being. Keep going; it won't take much longer.

Additionally, to come closer to self-actualization, I encourage anyone with deep secrets (hint: we all do) to spend some time uncovering them by writing about their lives. Like my friend mentioned in the preface, I'm sure you have some incredibly interesting things to share with the rest of us. I can't wait to hear about some of your personal and family secrets. Perhaps writing a book like this offers an alternative (or augmentation) to therapy, so you don't even need to share it with others for it to provide you with some value.

CHAPTER 4

Dad

My relationship with my father wasn't contentious, but there were times of contention. Many of the things that separated us died when he died, and with time, I have found strong emotions attached to the clashes he and I had have faded into obscurity. Equally, positive emotions surrounding our relationship have grown to near flawlessness now that he's gone. He was not a saint, despite how I tend to frame things more than a decade after his death. I know from the studies related to my undergraduate major in psychology that it's common for those who grieve the loss of a loved one to sanctify the memory of those who have passed. I realize I'm doing this in some instances, and where necessary, I put special effort into simply accepting the experiences without the need to repaint the memories or my feelings to put a better light on the topic.

That being said, the relationship I had with Dad was five parts fear, ten parts respect, and eighty-five parts love. I clearly recognize that my experiences with Dad will not comport with others' experiences with him, so I anticipate others may have some difficulty accepting the reliability of some of my stories.

I remain burdened with a couple of memories of the last two years of my father's life that are excruciatingly difficult for me to manage all these years after his passing. First, Dad was a lifelong smoker. I think he told me this habit began in his preteens, and he was never able to shake it, even in the face of developing emphysema or chronic obstructive pulmonary disease (COPD), like others in his family had. When my sister Deanne passed away in 2010, Dad began to exhibit what I passed off as simple anxiety about losing his youngest child (as if there is actually anything simple about this). I encouraged him to look into counseling to help cope with the stresses that came along with such an unexpected heartbreak.

He would call to tell me he was having trouble breathing, and upon my arrival at his house, I would dependably find him outside sitting in the garage (his favorite place), smoking and fidgeting in a lounge chair. Despite medical professionals diagnosing Dad with COPD and other heart-related issues, I refused to accept the connection between these diagnoses and his symptoms. Instead, I focused on something I knew was manageable, if not reversible, his anxiety. Dad's breathing continued to degrade over the next couple of years to the point that he was sent home after one hospital visit with oxygen tanks and a cannula line that would stretch the length of the house.

I was the one who transported Dad from his last stay at Athens Regional Hospital in late 2011 to his home in Statham, Georgia. It was then that the medical team explained there was nothing more they could do for him. They described hospice care and how he would need it when he returned home to help him be comfortable. Again, not being mentally prepared to let my father go, I immediately rationalized that hospice was ordered to allow Dad to convalesce from his latest bout of anxiety without having any out-of-pocket expenses. After all, the medical staff knew my parents were not able to afford rehabilitation co-pays. I never acknowledged Dad's true diagnosis, and certainly not his grim prognosis.

I feel guilty to this day with the thought that he may have felt as if I was minimizing his plight. Worse yet, I worry my insistence that his situation was *all in his head* may have made him feel like I thought he was weak or even crazy. In my regular discussions with him now, I repeatedly tell him I'm sorry for doing this, and I only hope he knows how badly I wanted the last couple of years of his life to simply be a hiccup in his fight to overcome these challenges and continue to physically be here with us all.

In the decades before his health declined, Dad was a serial entrepreneur. He dabbled in anything he either thought would make him fabulously wealthy or that he clearly enjoyed. Obviously, he never became a titan of business. I think he came to recognize he would never find himself on the cover of *Forbes Magazine* as one of the richest people on the planet, as he used to tell me his goal was to enjoy his time on earth and bounce his last check. So hoarding money wasn't his true goal. Mom said many times over the years that Dad would spend money as soon as he got it as if it was burning a hole in his pocket. Whether it was to go out to dinner, take a vacation, or buy a new car (or more likely a truck), I found Mom's statement to be more true than not. Illustrating how Dad used money as a tool (in this case humor, and perhaps a little nudge at Mom), he restored a truck and had me paint the inscription "Daddy's Dream…Momma's Money" on the tailgate.

I don't have many memories of Dad from the first ten years or so of my life. He seemed to be away from home a lot when we were young, working long hours as the general manager of a car dealership, for which he had a daily commute one way of about thirty miles. In fact, the first memory I have of my father belly-laughing was in about 1978 as the family was watching the weekly antics of Robin Williams on the sitcom *Mork & Mindy*. Despite working long hours as a salesman, he did find time to coach the football and baseball teams for which Robby and I played, and he was almost always home on Sundays. So, there are limited memories of Dad being around, mostly related to playing sports or getting together with relatives for Sunday lunch cookouts or early dinners. But for the most part, Dad was busy working a good bit in my early years. His absence didn't prevent me from growing close to him; in fact, it probably added to the connection. And I was often reminded that I would "be in big trouble when Dad gets home" whenever I did something one of my siblings or Mother didn't appreciate. Luckily, I was usually in bed when he made it home, and he was rarely afforded the opportunity to provide me with the promised discipline.

I looked up to him in many ways, mostly because he was my father, and growing up he was the smartest person I knew. Despite never having graduated high school, Dad just seemed to instinctively know how to do things, or at least had the confidence to try. He was handy around the house and could fix just about anything mechanical on a car. As automakers introduced increasingly complicated electronic innovations in the late 1970s, he recognized these modernizations surpassed his capacity. It was about this time in the evolution of automobile ingenuity that I decided I could afford a new car (1984). When I sought his counsel on what accessories I should consider, he said, "Avoid anything with fuel injection or electric windows and locks. These are just something else that can go wrong." I took his advice and bought a 1984 Camaro Z28 with a carbureted 305 with manual windows and locks. He was right, as not once did the windows, locks, or carburetor fail.

So much did I look up to my father that I asked him to be the best man at my wedding to Tracey in 1990. It was an auspicious opportunity for me to show Dad how much he meant to me without actually saying a word. I am the proverbial apple that hasn't fallen too far from the tree, as I would rather show someone what they mean to me than verbalize it. So I hope he accepted this invitation because he wanted to say back to me, "I love you too."

Dad's Family and the Complicated Relationships Borne by Deception

Dad grew up the youngest of seven children in the Ogburn family. He was preceded by Lewis, Sarah, Charles, Bill, Russ, and Jan. For reasons that are now obvious, we weren't particularly close with all of Dad's family. His parents were gone well before I was born, but we had a good number of opportunities to spend time with some of Dad's siblings at family reunions or during impromptu visits in one of our homes. Dad had very good relationships with Uncles Bill and Russ, and I recall a very loving and accepting atmosphere whenever we were around Uncle Lewis and his wife, Jimmie Sue. I once asked Dad what his father was like, to which the entirety of his response was, "Good as gold." I was probably around fourteen or so when I made this inquiry, so my youth is partially to blame for the failure to engage him in more specifics. The look on his face and the tenderness of his response allowed me a brief window into his relationship with his father. I also felt a little uncomfortable probing too deeply for fear that he wouldn't be able to emotionally employ me in further conversation about someone he seemed to truly love.

It was always a welcome occurrence for Mom and Dad to put the four of us (again, Deanne wasn't around yet) into the car for the short jaunt to Uncle Lewis and Aunt Jimmie's house in Decatur, Georgia. While the adults spent hours talking around the kitchen table, my siblings and I would join our cousins, Louie, Linda, and Little Jimmy, bounding about the house, banging on the piano, or generally making enough noise to cause consternation in the adults in the kitchen. These disruptions would inevitably result in Aunt Jimmie threatening to "get the army belt" to bring order (and, more importantly, quiet) back to the house. You see, the *army belt* accompanied Uncle Lewis back from his time in the service and was a force majeure to any disturbance, whether it be an invading opponent or a six-year-old trying to play a loud musical instrument for which he had no formal training.

The army belt was often mentioned but never observed. Despite never having seen it, we were all terrified by the descriptions, which seemed to grow more intimidating whenever our outbursts would return. By the time we would leave their house, we all had various ideas of what the army belt was, but we were all sure it had appurtenances attached that would rip enough flesh from our backsides to the point that sitting would be impossible for the rest of our lives. Looking back on this now, I know the army belt was just a deterrent and the threat was more humor to the adults than it was a true instrument they would use. We'll never really know, as just the mention of it put us all in line in every instance. To this day, the mention of the army belt in our family immediately quiets the room.

I think I was about six or seven at the time of one visit to Aunt Jimmie's house (Uncle Lewis had already passed away by this time) that, I realize now, may have had more influence on me than I would have ever known. After being threatened with the army belt several times, all the children were sent to different parts of the house and told to find something quiet to do. Being about a half-century past, I don't recall the specifics of what was happening to prevent us from being banished to the outdoors to burden the rest of the neighborhood with our clamor. Nonetheless, we decided to calm tensions between the generations by playing a board game in the living room (dangerously close to the calling piano). While everyone else congregated on the floor of the living room, I followed Little Jimmy to his room to choose a board game for the awaiting contestants.

At the time, I shared a bedroom with Robby back at our house and we had very little room to store things. So we shoved all of our toys and other belongings into the closet and a small toy box whenever we were instructed to clean up our room. Back in Little Jimmy's room, I was astonished, nay, flabbergasted and speechless when I witnessed him go underneath his bed to retrieve some very organized stacks of boxed games. I don't recall which game we chose to play, but I do remember his world of organization began to assault my senses that day. It was finally clear that we had options beyond chaotically throwing things into a closet or toy box. Not only did I now have additional space to store things (we thought putting things under our beds was unacceptable since the specific charge was to "clean up and get everything off the floor"), but if I approached storage with a bit more forethought, I could potentially get more out of my space. Marie Kondo would have been proud. And it is satisfactory to take advantage of space under the bed, even if that means something stays on the floor. So it may come as a surprise to Little Jimmy (we call him Jim now) that he played a big part in the development of my obsessive-compulsive tendencies.

As I mentioned earlier, Dad had strong bonds with Uncles Bill and Russ. We had lots of interactions with them over the years and it was clear that Dad was devastated when the two of them passed away, at different times and under different circumstances. Uncle Bill was a jokester and loved everyone hard. The incredibly lasting memories I have of Uncle Bill are of the times he would come to our house on Sunday mornings for breakfast. I was too young to know the circumstances of his visits, but I know they were always welcome and his presence was always positive. Because he loved big breakfasts, we would venture outside the normal pattern of having cereal and toast on the days he visited us. Therefore, the smell of bacon and grits is attached to my fond memories of Uncle Bill to this day.

One thing Uncle Bill left me with was the ability to skillfully drop-kick a football. It hasn't been a terribly useful skill in the grand scheme of things, but I am proud to say that my uncle Bill taught me how to do this. Despite the relative uselessness of this skill, I wish I had passed it down to my son Nicholas.

Uncle Russ was closest in age to Dad, save Aunt Jan, and Dad bore a very strong physical resemblance to Russ. Dad genuinely loved Russ; they got together a lot and talked on the phone even more. They worked together at the *Atlanta Journal* and played on the journal's bowling team together in the early 1960s. My recollections of Russ are clearer than those I have of either Bill or Lewis, as Lewis died in April of 1969, when I was four, and Bill died in June of 1972 when I was seven. Russ passed away in February of 2001; therefore, I had more time with him since I was in my mid-thirties when he passed away.

Uncle Russ had a lazy eye, but it didn't seem to impair him in any way. Whenever he came to our house, we would inevitably end up outside throwing the baseball—I have no idea why, but it was something we both enjoyed doing. I was always overly conscious of Russ' eye, and I was terrified to throw the ball when I wasn't completely sure he was looking my way. So much was my hesitation to throw the ball one day (I hesitated about fifteen seconds longer than normal), Russ yelled, "Throw the goddamn ball, I *am* looking at you!" Russ, like Bill, was funny and his self-deprecating humor always mitigated the tension of a situation. Like Dad, I will continue to miss Bill and Russ until the day I die, but I am incredibly thankful for the memories they both provided me.

Uncle Charles was an enigma to me. He was a very tall man (six feet five or thereabout, as I recall), and his size was intimidating for me, as was his quiet demeanor whenever I was in his presence. He never seemed to be interested in our family. It's not that he was hostile, but he just wasn't around very much, and I don't remember ever having talked with him. There was a time in which I needed his help, and he delivered the needed assistance without hesitation… after all, we were *family*.

In the 1980s, Uncle Charles held the title of fire chief for the city of Valdosta, Georgia. His tenure in this position serendipitously lined up with my pilot training at Embry-Riddle Aeronautical University in Daytona Beach, Florida. In October of 1982, I was required to perform a solo cross-country flight to provide experience toward my Private Pilot License. Not of any consequence, but I piloted a 1982 Cessna 172 Skyhawk, with the tail number N92ER. I had only racked up a total of 41.2 flight hours up to this point and had performed my first solo flight on August 12 of that year, but I was confident and absolutely ecstatic to take a long trip without anyone sharing the cockpit of this très petit plane. The cockpit of a C-172 is roughly the size of the interior of a subcompact car, smaller than a Toyota Corolla. These planes are so small that you need to step outside if you want to change your mind. Confined areas like these do not comfort me when I must share the space with others. So having this time and space to myself for the roughly eight-hour excursion was exciting to an introvert like me.

My chosen route was to take me from Daytona Beach, Florida, to Savannah, Georgia, to Valdosta, Georgia, and then back to Daytona Beach before the sun set as I wasn't yet rated to fly solo at night. A schoolmate of mine had chosen the same route for his cross-country flight, and we decided to meet up at each stop to keep an eye out for one another. I landed in Savannah first and proceeded to refuel my plane while I waited for my classmate. He was about a half hour behind me, and therefore, I took off from Savannah and headed for Valdosta with the same lead time.

I arrived at the Valdosta airport right on schedule, but my friend didn't show up at his expected arrival time. I had been in touch with flight operations at Embry-Riddle and they were getting worried, as they had not heard from air traffic control that my fellow pilot had landed within his expected window. So they asked me to stay put and wait for him there. It turns out my classmate had overshot Valdosta by failing to read his instruments correctly, only to have air traffic control guide him from the *big lake* he saw in his windscreen back to Valdosta. He touched down about three hours later just as the sun was setting, meaning it was too late for us to get in the air and back to Daytona Beach without breaking the rules of engagement.

So we were stuck in Valdosta, Georgia, for the night with nowhere to sleep unless we found a corner of the small airport to claim as our sleeping quarters. After a quick call to Dad, my friend and I were picked up from the airport by a firetruck and whisked away to one of the nearby fire stations in the thriving metropolis of Azalea City: Valdosta, Georgia. Uncle Charles had coordinated the pickup and rallied the crew to welcome us in with dinner cooked and delivered by the community. I have no idea how much he put into this, but the firemen on duty that night told us that my Uncle Charles pulled out all the stops for the family. I didn't see Uncle Charles that night or the next morning when the crew drove us back to the airport in the firetruck. After a night of feeling somewhat like a celebrity, my classmate and I were on our way again. This time, I instructed my classmate to take my wing, as I didn't want to find that he was again staring down Lake Superior in his attempt to get back home. About two hours later, we landed at DAB and debriefed flight operations while everyone laughed about the big lake he observed, which was actually the Gulf of Mexico.

I mentioned earlier that Aunt Jan was close in age to Dad. However, she moved to Minnesota with her family sometime before I was able to form many memories with her. However, there always seemed to be respect and affection between Aunt Jan and Dad.

I'm sorry to say that because of the distance between Georgia and Minnesota, I don't have any significant memories of Aunt Jan.

In contrast to the relationships with all of his other siblings, Dad always seemed to be beholden to his eldest sister Sarah (we called her Aunt Tay). We would go to her house in the West End neighborhood of Atlanta at least a couple of times a year to celebrate Christmas and other occasional holidays or family birthdays. My memories of Aunt Tay are relegated mostly to the physical aspects of her house and the feeling she did not enjoy our presence all that much. Tay's house on Lawton Street was a small bungalow-type home with two bedrooms, one bath, a small living room, a small dining area, and a small galley kitchen that led to a stoop in the backyard. Her husband, having died before any memories of him were filed away into my hippo-campus, left Aunt Tay living there alone for many of the years as I grew up, save for some time when our great-aunt Bessie Bissell (we knew her as Bebo) shared the house with her. Nonetheless, I suspect the house was comfortable for one or two people, but shoehorn-ing another two adults and four children under the age of ten likely frayed Tay's nerves. So we were constantly shushed and reprimanded for what we felt were insignificant behaviors, like talking too loudly, racing our Matchbox cars on the hardwood floors, or trying to sneak pieces of hard candy that seemed to be permanently fused together by the sugar coating and aggregating dust from the previous decade or so. Many times we were chased outside by Tay to "do something productive," which inevitably meant we needed to straighten up the miscellaneous things in her backyard or spend the afternoon raking leaves. I know our *productivity* in the backyard had no bearing on maintaining her home but was a way to get us out of the house to return her to the quiet she had enjoyed before our arrival.

The only other lasting memory I have of Aunt Tay was the silver Christmas tree she displayed every year, adorned with the requisite tricolored light wheel that rotated the hue of the silver thistles of the tree from red to green to yellow. It was spectacular to a child of four or five, but as time passed, I began to see this as a tacky accoutrement for the holiday. Like many things, though, I see nostalgia has rein-vigorated the silver tree market, and what is old is new again. Based on my experiences, though, I choose to avoid reigniting the negative memories that have attached themselves to the silver tree on Lawton Street.

I mentioned earlier that Dad grew up the youngest of seven children. Well, that wasn't exactly the story. Mom and Dad didn't have much time (or money) to take trips, just the two of them, early in their marriage, as they both needed to work to maintain the family that began growing approximately eleven months after they wed. However, in 1986, they decided to splurge and take a cruise to Mexico to celebrate their twenty-eighth wedding anniversary. As part of the travel requirements, they had to secure a copy of their birth certificates to prove citizenship upon their return to the US. It is interesting that Dad never needed a copy of his birth certificate before he was in his forties, but that's not pertinent to this story.

Upon reviewing his birth certificate, Dad learned that his entire upbringing was a ruse. He uncovered the reality that the person he thought was his sister Sarah (our Aunt Tay) was actually his birth mother. It was not a terribly uncommon thing in the 1930s to have a child outside of marriage, but it was still considered a stain on the family to have such a thing happen. So like many families of the time, having a young and unmarried daughter become pregnant resulted in an elaborate effort to conceal the situation to avoid embarrassing the family. The two people Dad grew up knowing as his parents delivered Sarah to relatives in South Carolina to gestate the pregnancy outside the view of friends, neighbors, and the younger siblings. At the end of her pregnancy, Sarah returned to Atlanta to deliver her child unceremoniously at St. Joseph's Hospital. When Dad was born, he was brought into the home as the youngest child of Walter Edward and Mary Frances (Mamie) Bissell Ogburn. Sarah would spend the next four decades posing as my father's eldest sister.

We've since learned that several of my father's "siblings" (those closest to Sarah's age) knew the real story, but the younger ones were shielded from the truth for all these years. Russ, Jan, and Tay were the only living "siblings" when Dad discovered the truth, so he didn't have a chance to reestablish relationships with the others as a nephew rather than a brother. Jan was still living in Minnesota and interactions with Dad were very limited, so I am unaware of how this new factor affected her relationship with Dad. However, learning Dad's true place in the family only strengthened his connection to Russ. Russ continued to treat Dad as his little brother until the day he died. The fact that Russ treated Dad, and the rest of us for that matter, the same after the revelation only strengthened the respect and love I have for Russ.

Tay's relationships with me, my siblings, and our mother didn't really change, as she continued to be harsh with us and treated us with what constantly felt to be disdain or, still worse, animosity. Mom has opined over the years that Tay treated us the way she did because she didn't want others to think she had any sort of partiality to us because it would illuminate her true maternal link through her first (and ultimately only) child. If this is true, Tay definitely overcompensated (from my perspective) by treating all the other children in the family much better than she did us. Once the truth was exposed, Tay seemed to expect Dad to suddenly become her son and do things for her that she had never asked of him in the past. For Dad's part, he attempted to warm to the idea of having a mother this late in his life, as the mother he knew for his first forty-seven years actually passed away when he was just sixteen.

No doubt related to the many guilt trips Tay laid upon him, Dad began to feel like he was somehow responsible for taking care of her as she aged—this, despite her absolute inability to be a mother to him in any way. One thing she could have done to provide some degree of solace to Dad would have been to apologize for not being there for him for all these years…she never did that. And she took the name of his biological father to her grave despite being asked many times so as to provide us all with some degree of closure or at least some ability to trace back basic information on family health histories.

This entire affair profoundly affected Dad. Prior to this, he was a reasonably self-assured person with a confident outward appearance. Afterward, he became more sullen and less resilient to challenges, as he wasn't sure of anything if he could be deceived for so many years about something so central to his identity. Dad's entire experience would likely have been very different had he come home as the first grandchild of the family rather than the last child of aging parents. Again, this book isn't intended to analyze Dad's experience, but this newly defined place in the Ogburn family affected the rest of my immediate family in many ways.

I won't speak for anyone else, but I can say without any reservations that my relationship with Tay was never very strong and only became more strained after learning her true connection to my father (and by extension, to me). My relationship with Aunt Tay was permanently severed when I was in college in the late 1980s. I was struggling to make enough money to pay for my car, gas, and books for school, and one year was only able to muster enough cash to buy my mother a card for her birthday. After learning I hadn't provided anything beyond the card, Tay orated that she "would wipe [her] ass with the card and throw it out." Being someone uncomfortable with confrontation, especially ones that have little upside, I chose to quietly avoid her in all possible situations for the remainder of her life. She did attend my wedding in 1990 and was seated as my grandmother. However, it was out of respect for my father that I obliged her request to be so honored. I do not recall speaking with her that day, and two weeks after our wedding, Tracey and I moved away to Fort Lauderdale to begin my career in public health. This offered me the physical distance to avoid any possible interactions with her altogether. I did not attend her funeral.

It may seem that I hold some enmity toward her, but it would more aptly be described as apathy. I don't necessarily hold a grudge toward her, but I do recognize how her actions affected my father (and the entire family). I've accepted the situation and understand that the relationships I have with the remaining Ogburn family members are mine through Dad's place in the family and not through Tay's. They accept us without condition or any expectancy of difference between being first or second cousins. So I'm extraordinarily proud to be part of the Ogburn extended cousin group.

A little additional genealogic sleuthing uncovered a couple of other interesting Ogburn family facts. Aunt Tay's pregnancy wasn't the first one in the family that was nontraditional. It seems that Mary

Frances (the woman Dad believed was his mother for many years) also became pregnant before she was married to Walter. Walter was drafted into the service and fought in the war before returning to the States to find Mary Frances pregnant with his child and living in a small community in north Georgia about 100 miles northeast of Atlanta. Family lore surmises that Mary Frances was sent to Habersham County to avoid the same family shame that her first daughter would suffer years later. Upon his return from the war, Walter quickly tracked Mary Frances down, married her, and shortly thereafter, the newlywed couple welcomed Lewis as their first child. This isn't so much a family secret, but just a detail that no one feels is important, as Walter and Mary Frances were happily married and raised a family without any concerns for the timing of the arrival of their first offspring. They remained married until Mary Frances died in 1956.

I've described above the house that Aunt Tay lived in on Lawton Street when I was young. It was, in fact, the same house that Walter and Mary Frances lived in with their young family in the 1930s and 1940s. My best guess on this house is that it encompassed no more than about 1,200 square feet. Incredibly, the 1940 Census placed thirty-two souls living in this structure. How they were able to get thirty-two people into that house, much less sleep and share a single bathroom, is beyond me. This fact alone now gives me a little more appreciation for why Aunt Tay was frazzled when we came to visit her...after all, she was probably still a bit shell-shocked from having shared that same space with thirty-one other human beings just twenty-five years before. I would likely have some PTSD from that experience as well.

CHAPTER 5

I Never Realized Dad Was a Genius Until He Died

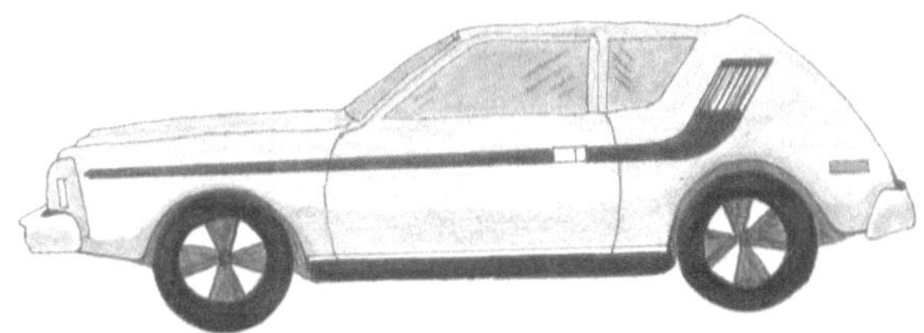

Like most children, when I was growing up, I thought my parents were morons. They provided us with all the necessities of life and everything, but they always seemed to make the wrong decisions and do things that I would never have done. They embarrassed me with their jokes, their hairstyles, the way they dressed…on and on. I'm not proud that this is how I felt at the time, as they were good people trying to raise a family in strange and challenging times. It's been said thousands of times that there is no instruction book for raising kids, so we all just wing it and hope for the best.

Life experiences have taught me lots of things, one of which is that I was the moron and my parents were making great decisions on things that I had no way of comprehending at such a young age. They were winging it, but they managed to raise five reasonably well-adjusted adults who have each contributed to society in a variety of positive ways. I am introspective by nature, so I've come to appreciate most of the things my parents provided to us in our upbringing. I continue to question why we had to eat liver every so often, but most of the other things make sense now that I'm an adult (and a parent).

Having children of my own allowed me to appreciate the difficulties of transiting through life while keeping the train on the tracks. Looking back now, I can point to a number of things my dad did or said that affected me in positive ways. Aggregating these stories now leads me to believe that he was a genius in lots of ways. I didn't know it until I lost his physical presence, but I regularly hear his voice now reminding me how to approach things when I'm faced with challenges.

Dad had a story about nearly everything…I think this is where I get it. Most of his stories had a significant point to make, even if you couldn't figure it out right away. So in a way, Dad was a teacher, and his children were his students. Occasionally, the lessons were about business, other times they were about safety, and still others were about religion/faith. I suspect some of his lessons were also just ways he could amuse himself at our expense.

Faith/Religion

One of Dad's lessons is one I've heard in several different forms over the years. I'm sure Dad didn't come up with this anecdote, but it was impactful enough on me to take it to heart and use it to my advantage over the years. The general lesson he offered in this particular scenario is about taking advantage of opportunities when they present themselves, and more importantly, not to sit back and wait for things to just fall into your lap. One fable oft recounted was the one about the faithful woman caught in a flood. It goes something like this:

The forecast called for heavy rain over the next several days, and subsequent flooding was all but certain. So the fire department went around town alerting residents of the need to evacuate to higher ground. When they came across this woman sitting on her porch, they explained the situation and offered to get her to safety. However, her response was, "No, thank you, as God is my protector, and he will provide for me." As the rain continued and the flood waters rose, the woman found herself having to retreat to the second story of her home. The fire department returned to her house in a boat. Again, they offered to take her to safety, and she restated her refusal, saying, "No, thank you, as God is my protector, and he will provide for me." The next morning, the flood waters rose still further, causing the woman to move onto the roof of her house to escape the water. Again, the fire department came this time using a helicopter. Unsurprisingly, she responded again with, "No, thank you, as God is my protector, and he will provide for me." The waters continued to rise, and the woman was swept away to her death. When she made it to the gates of heaven, she cried to Saint Peter, "Why has God forsaken me?" Saint Peter replied that she had not been forsaken, as God sent the fire department with their truck, then with a boat, and finally with a helicopter.

A second story Dad used to tell with the same lesson was about a young father having trouble providing for his family. In fact, the family was about to be evicted from their home because they couldn't pay the rent. So every day, the man asked God to let him win the lottery so his family wouldn't be evicted. Each week, the numbers were drawn, and the man didn't win. This went on for several months, and the man gave up on ever winning the lottery. Finally, after being evicted, the man asked God why he didn't win. God responded to the man with, "You've got to meet me halfway and buy a ticket." The moral of these two stories is that faith is more successful if you (1) take advantage of what God provides and (2) take the initiative to meet God halfway.

While Dad was a salesman, I definitely am not. I am not comfortable with the uncertainty of not knowing when the next sale is coming. I think his many years in the car business provided him with the ability to see through the lean times, and he used to tell me, "Don't worry about the money. It will always come." I have always been a worrier about finances, but having the last thirty-plus years on which to reflect, he was right. I've had times when we had less than I'd like, but something always comes along when you need it the most. Bonuses have come when I wasn't sure how to manage through some tight financial situations. It's almost like there is some larger plan being played out of which I'm not aware, but the money always comes. Dad wasn't a terribly religious person, but I think this statement was his way of showing he had faith in God to provide what he and his family needed (and when). Again, while sustenance is important, I'm still trying to find out if eating liver is really part of God's plan.

Wish and *Spit*

Somewhat connected to these stories is a saying I heard from Dad on way too many occasions. While Dad was a dreamer, he lived long enough to know that success wasn't going to knock on your door uninvited. Many times when I would start a sentence with "I wish" or "I hope," Dad would cut me off to tell me to recount the long-held axiom: "Wish in one hand and spit (cleaned up for sensitive audiences) in the other. See which one fills up first." So it's better to take action than to wait for success to come. I call the alternative, passive approach *backing into success*. Sure, it is technically possible (but not probable) that you might get lucky and have someone just hand you keys to a new car without asking for payment, but it's not at all probable! Besides, you're not likely to appreciate the car in the same way as if you had worked hard for it in the first place. And besides, having things given to you without providing any effort doesn't exude any skill or determination on your part to account for the achievement.

To this day, I advocate (both in my personal and professional lives) that you should identify your goals and the steps it will take to achieve them, and then take action to make progress toward them. You'll get there faster if you're moving toward them rather than waiting for them to come to you. This adage comes into play as a motivator in my planning to make someone pay for the pain they inflicted on me and my family. So rather than hoping karma might catch up to them, I decided to put effort into how and when retribution would be delivered. More on that later…

Efficiency

Dad had a way of imparting his wisdom (even if it was a cliché) by connecting it to my daily activities—teaching moments if you will. When I was working on my undergraduate degree at Oglethorpe University in Atlanta, I was employed at my father's used car lot and body shop a few short miles away to earn some spending money. I was part of a small crew of car detailers that Dad put together to have a third income stream using the same business footprint. Many of the cars we brought in for cleaning were trade-ins from other auto dealers in the area, and I was mainly responsible for doing the *wet work* (washing the body, engine, and undercarriage of the cars). Once the wet work was finished, I delivered the cars to others on the team who would polish the outside and clean the interior. I had a habit of scouring the cars for loose change before releasing them to the others in the detailing chain. Much to the consternation of my teammates and Dad, this would sometimes take an hour or two (removing seats and door panels is time-consuming).

Rather than telling me that "time is money" and hoping I would just stop doing this, Dad had me count the change I had found each time and account for the time it took to liberate said change for a week. At the end of the week, I was able to bank several dollars in "free" money, but the amount of time it took to secure this money cost us about eight hours of lost productivity. Dad then explained that losing a full day's work for five or six dollars in change actually cost us about $180, as we could usually clean about three cars in that amount of time. Anytime I would revert back to this practice, Dad would say something along the lines of "You're fixing a $5 problem with a $180 solution."

After having worked for the US government for more than thirty years now, I can say that I have tried to impart this exact same lesson to hundreds of others by saying, "Let's not continue to solve $10,000 problems with $100,000 solutions." It works sometimes, and other times it falls on deaf ears. Nonetheless, it is a saying I've recounted so many times (and to so many colleagues) that I suspect it will continue to live on at the CDC well after I've retired.

Leadership

After classes at Oglethorpe ended one day, I arrived for my shift and found Dad had a task waiting for me to accomplish before I changed into my work clothes. While I was at school that morning, someone else on the detailing team had to do the wet work on a Corvette that arrived earlier in the day. Unfortunately, they used a chemical on the aluminum wheels that removed the plastic coating on the wheels, causing them to become very cloudy. This was a semi-catastrophic event that, without some serious (and immediate) remediation, would result in the wheels being a total loss.

After Dad explained the situation, he sent me to the customer's workplace, a Chrysler store about a mile away, to try and make things right. I arrived at the customer's office only to have the used car manager berate me as if I were the *idiot* who ruined the wheels. I tried to convince him we had the tools and materials to salvage the wheels, but he was belligerent and unwilling to give us a chance to make amends. In fact, the customer completely cut ties with us and said he would never do business with us again. I was devastated and cried on my way back to the shop, thinking I had failed Dad and the rest of the team.

Dad helped me understand there was nothing I could have done to rescue this situation and that I had done exactly what he wanted me to do:

1. proceed face-forward into a situation I knew was going to be difficult;
2. accept responsibility for the mistake that *we* made;
3. not blame any individual for the failure; and
4. give the customer a person to whom to direct their anger and not allow them to confront any of our team members directly

I was not there to maintain a business relationship but to do all I could to show our team we had their backs and would not throw them to the wolves over an honest mistake.

Word got around to many of our other clients, and our relationships with them were strengthened because of the way we faced this head-on and accepted responsibility. I heard from one of our other main clients (a Chevrolet dealership) that they thought while we made a mistake with the wheels, the folks at the Chrysler store were wrong to end the business relationship and treat us in such a harsh manner. There is some consolation that the Chevy store is still in business all these years later and the Chrysler store is now a buffet-style Chinese restaurant…I don't hold a grudge, though.

Integrity in the Working World

I've tried to describe my father to people who didn't know him, and I have a few attributes that seem to do the trick. I've termed Dad a serial entrepreneur. He tried lots of things in his life, even when they were not familiar. He raced cars, owned car lots, gas stations, auto body shops, pawn shops, a flea market, and even a trophy/engraving shop. He was a dreamer and was generally optimistic in his outlook on how these businesses would fare. He had a habit of jumping in without a safety net, and most of his businesses had a short lifespan. He wasn't afraid to take on things that were unfamiliar, and in absolutely every instance he learned something.

While making tons of money would have been great, I think Dad was more interested in doing something that allowed others to succeed. He had many opportunities to take advantage of people (and no doubt did so on occasion), but he seemed to be a sucker for the underdog or for those down on their luck. I've seen him go into a partnership with someone because they had come into hard times and couldn't pull themselves out of the hole…he helped them out of their situation while putting himself on the line. I've also seen him give people who owed him money a pass because he knew they had a family to support. There's no doubt in my mind he would have been financially successful if he had taken the cold approach to business.

I find myself to be humanistic in most areas of my life because of how Dad approached his businesses. I think this attribute has contributed to my success…I'm not rich, but I can sleep at night knowing that I am not taking advantage of people just for a buck.

Work Ethic

Mom used to say Dad could sell an icebox to an Eskimo. I've witnessed this firsthand, and I never really understood how good he was precisely because he was so good at it. When I was in college, I worked with Dad in a couple of his businesses. One summer we sold boats and motorhomes at Andy's in Marietta, Georgia, where Dad was the general manager. He taught me that every customer comes in with the intention to buy something, and all you need to do is provide them with accurate information and treat them like they're the only thing you're focused on. Pay attention to names and talk with them, not at them. Even if they don't buy something from you right then, they're more likely to come back for something later if you treat them like a friend.

I remember one customer who came in to *just look* at the motorhomes. We sold Winnebago motorhomes, and they were at the top of the price point at the time. So, we had lots of lookers who would come in to compare and then go buy a less expensive option at another store. One afternoon Dad sent me out to talk with this fellow, and it turned out to be what I thought was a waste of time, as I didn't make a sale. I followed Dad's rules: I answered all of the customer's questions and simply had a nice conversation with him. Well, a couple of weeks later, the customer called back and talked with Dad to say he was going to buy the thirty-seven-foot Winnebago I showed him. He liked the fact that I answered his questions and didn't try any pressure tactics that he experienced at another Winnebago dealership closer to his home. I didn't know at the time, but this fellow was a retired physician, and he paid the entire $97,000 in cash. I didn't sell him anything; he bought it.

To this day, I talk with people (not at/to them) and make sure I am focused on them by not getting distracted by phone calls, texts, or other interruptions when we're together. Many times, I've had phone calls come in while in meetings with someone in my office, only to have them ask if I wanted to take the call. Every time this happens, my response is the same: "No, I can get back to them. Taking advantage of the time I have with you now is important to me." I don't check the phone to see who is calling, and I think this adds to the credence of my commitment to them.

Innovation

Dad was working at Bill Spreen Toyota in Atlanta in 1973 when, one afternoon, he came up with an idea to draw people into the dealership. He suggested the dealership have a couple of baseball players from the Atlanta Braves come in for a meet-and-greet with fans and sign a few baseballs. This wasn't unheard of at the time, but it wasn't terribly common back in 1973. What was different here was that the Atlanta Braves in the early 1970s had a couple of future Hall of Famers on the roster, but the team struggled to win just about 50 percent of their games. Well, Dad was able to get these two future Hall of Famers (Hank Aaron and Phil Niekro) to make an appearance at the dealership.

Dad brought home three signed baseballs that day, two autographed by Hank Aaron and one signed by Phil Niekro. The Niekro ball was signed to me and Robby, and it holds a special place in Robby's collection to this day. I was fortunate enough to meet Phil a couple of times over the years, and one time I was proud to introduce Nicholas to him. He was so gracious and signed a few things for Nicholas and pulled him onto his lap for a few photos. About two years before Phil passed away (several after Dad had himself passed), I met Phil again before a Braves game in Atlanta. I recounted the time Dad had him come to the dealership for a signing, and his response was, "Bill Spreen Toyota. Man, that was a long time ago."

Dad gave me and Robby each one of the Hank Aaron balls. These balls signed by Hank Aaron are unique for a lot of reasons but namely because they are embellished with the Atlanta Braves emblem of the time and because they were signed before Hank became the all-time home run king just a few short months afterward. This ball is proudly displayed in my home to remind me of my father more than Hank Aaron, although it sure is nice to know that Hank is another connection I had with my father. A few years before Dad died, I told him I wouldn't give up this ball for anything in the world…not even $10,000. He was flabbergasted and responded, "Boy, you've got to be crazy." To which my retort was that the ball is special, not because of the man who signed it, but because of the man who gave it to me.

Money Management

Dad never held a job long enough to get vested in an employer-sponsored retirement plan. I suspect he never thought he would live long enough to be able to retire, so managing money wasn't really his forte. As I mentioned earlier, he used to tell us his financial goal in life was to bounce his last check. It's ironic that he actually paid a debt to society earlier in his life for bouncing checks. Nonetheless, Dad didn't have an IRA or 401(k) plan set aside to assist in his golden years, as he planned to use the money he (and Mom) had before he passed away.

A joke the comedian Jeff Foxworthy tells in his stand-up routines reminds me of Dad. It goes something like: "Sophisticated people have retirement plans. Rednecks play the lottery." Well, I never thought of my dad as a card-carrying redneck, but he did play the lottery. A few days before Dad passed away, the family was gathered at his house trying to steal some moments of lucidity before his passing. At one point, Dad summoned my oldest sister Michele for what I surmise would be his last attempt to provide his family with an inheritance. He asked Michele to get his credit card out of his billfold and buy some lottery tickets. I am certain he knew he wouldn't be around to collect on any potential winnings, so I like to think he was just paying into his estate. And as was the pattern, his lottery numbers didn't get called on the last tickets he purchased.

Electricity

In the mid-1970s, Dad was the general manager for Andy's AMC/Jeep and Sports Car Center in Marietta, Georgia (yes, the same Andy who owned the Winnebago store). As one of the perks of his position, Dad bought a "Gremlin" go-cart for us to play with in our backyard. I have tons of very fond memories of this go-cart, mostly because it came with a fiberglass body in the shape of an AMC Gremlin. It was about one-tenth the size of a regular Gremlin and as such, there was a permanent sunroof that allowed even a ten-year-old to stick his head and shoulders out to see where he was going.

We had lots of fun driving that go-cart around the cul-de-sac behind our house. Without traffic, we were able to drive in circles unabated until the sun set (there were no headlights or street lights) or we ran out of gas. The baseball and football fields in the middle of the cul-de-sac were sacrosanct for the go-cart because, after all, we didn't want to scar up the base paths with tire tracks. The cul-de-sac (we called it the *turnaround*) had two challenging corners (sand and gravel traps), and the more we drove "the Gremlin," the better drivers we became while attempting to traverse these hazards. I don't have anything of real value I can place on these experiences except to say that I attribute my ability to deal with slick gravel and sand (and occasionally ice) while driving regular-sized automobiles to all my time driving the one-tenth-scale Gremlin. Considering the thousands of accidents I've had when coming across these types of hazards while driving full-sized automobiles, perhaps my education with the Gremlin in the turnaround wasn't as instructive as I originally considered.

Dad probably didn't see this as anything more than a way to keep us entertained (and out of the house) for long swaths of time. However, he did have one lesson to impart, and I was the direct recipient. The Gremlin go-cart was brand new when we got it, so we never had trouble cranking it (it was a pull-cord start, as electric starters for go-carts back in the 1970s were not terribly common). One day, Dad lifted the body of the go-cart to access the engine and acted as if there was something wrong. After a few minutes, Dad exclaimed, "Aha!" as he identified the issue as a loose spark plug wire. So he said the only way we could get it started was for me to hold the wire on the spark plug while he pulled the starting cord. I did as instructed, and Dad proceeded to pull the cord at what I realize now was a very short and slow attempt to create a minimum spark for the engine. Well, it was just enough to jolt me and send Dad and my brother Robby into a laughing fit that lasted until I was in the house, inconsolably upset, with my mother wondering why.

Later that day, when Mom was yelling at Dad for this, his response was that he was teaching us how to have respect for the inner workings of all things mechanical. I just remember him snickering, not sitting back in some sort of professorial stance, proud of the lesson he had imparted to a trusting student. I will say, though, that to this day I still have a lifelong respect (fear) for any amount of electricity. Oh, and I've never been severely injured by electricity. Thanks, Dad! Another lesson learned.

Growing Up

Sharp as a tack

As a child, I think most of us have an innate desire to live up to our parents' expectations. All the spankings I endured growing up didn't hurt nearly as much as when I felt like I had disappointed or let my parents down. In my experience, my mother was better at conveying her love for her children when we were young. She was more affectionate and told us she loved us more than Dad did, but somehow, we knew Dad loved and was proud of us. Dad would say, "Good job," when we did something that met his expectations, and I suspect he was very liberal in his "attaboys" as a way to express his love for us.

There are a couple of strong memories I have regarding Dad's words of affection to me when I was young. The night I graduated from kindergarten is one of those memories. After getting dressed in my very first Sears suit (replete with the obligatory clip-on tie) for the ceremony, with the long felt brown drapes of our living room as a backdrop, my mother snapped a picture of me in my cheap blue suit to memorialize the event. When Mom asked Dad what he thought of me in my *grown-up* suit, Dad said that I was "as sharp as a tack." It's funny how this comment still brings me to tears all these years later. As mentioned before, Mom was more affectionate to us, so hearing these tender words from my father was unexpected and infinitely gratifying.

Something equally impactful happened a few years later when I accompanied Dad to his workplace (Neil Pope Ford) in the mid-1970s. When we got to the dealership, we went inside and I stayed in his office as he continued on to the business office to retrieve his paycheck. One of Dad's coworkers saw me and came by to ask my name. When I told him, he immediately said, "Oh yeah, you're Mike's youngest son, aren't you? I hope you know that your dad is very proud of you." He didn't give me any specifics about why this was the case, but the fact that he knew by my name that I was the youngest son tells me Dad probably talked about us a good bit to his friends. Until that moment, I didn't know Dad ever talked about me (or any of his children) with anyone besides Mom.

Expanding World

Growing up in the late 1960s and early 1970s on the outskirts (at the time) of Atlanta, we were still living in a pretty homogeneous community. It was quite odd for us to be around anyone who didn't look like us and speak like we did. And we were occasionally exposed to others who didn't have as much as we did (although we didn't have all that much). So whenever we experienced those different from us, we reacted like most preteens tend to do…with naive ignorance.

A story I often, embarrassingly yet fondly, recount involves my introduction to a new student in my class who spoke Spanish. I was so enamored with this *new* language that I told Mom and Dad, "A little boy came to school today and spoke incursive." I've heard this same anecdote from others over the years, so I suspect, like many things, I was not the first person to ever think this. This particular story will likely generate some degree of recoil for some, but it reminds me of how sheltered we were and the youthful exuberance that comes from an innocent seven-year-old being offered a new experience.

I've mentioned before that I grew up in a humble home. And not having much to call our own, we were astute in keeping our possessions in the family. My mother used to have a small garden when we were growing up. Nothing major, just a few tomato plants, as I recall. One day, Robby came running into the house to alert everyone that *some little bastard* had just stolen some of Mom's tomatoes. Unlike most of the anecdotes in this book, I'm nearly certain this one was implanted in me by all the times the story has been recounted over the years in ways that were intended to (but never successful) embarrass Robby. I'm pretty sure the loss of a couple of tomatoes wasn't a nail in our financial coffin, but all these years later, this story reminds me that despite our ascetic means, there were others who had even less than we did. However, thanks to the way we were brought up, we were never aware that others had more. I thought nearly everyone shared the challenges of making ends meet, and therefore we had to be careful to make the most of what was afforded to us. To reiterate the point, I don't think I'm cheap, but I'm not going to let some little bastard steal my tomatoes! And I'm now just beginning to understand why I've been calling the squirrels that steal from our backyard bird feeder *little bastards*.

ESP

One day, Robby came home from elementary school with black paper covering his two front teeth. He explained that his teeth were knocked out during recess. I fell for it, and he had a good laugh. The next day, someone came up to me at school to tell me that Robby was checked out to go to the doctor, as he had an accident playing hockey at recess. They explained he had his front teeth knocked out when someone hit him in the mouth with a hockey stick. "Yeah, right. He tricked me with that yesterday," I responded. Well, it turned out he really did lose his teeth at recess that day.

No matter how many times I've explained Robby had tricked me the day before his accident, no one in my family (including Robby) has ever admitted this ever happened. So one of three things is going on here:

1. Robby really did do this, and he continues to lie about it all these years later;
2. It never happened, and I have somehow manufactured the memory to better accept the trauma; or
3. I had a premonition about Robby's accident.

First of all, Robby can keep a secret for a short period of time, but then he will eventually admit to the ruse. An example of his inability to stay true to the shtick long-term involves his playing a trick on our sister Michele many years later. You see, Michele has an aversion to eggshells…specifically having eggshells accidentally mixed in with deviled eggs. One year at Thanksgiving, Robby gave Michele a *tainted* deviled egg, resulting in the desired effect: Michele dry-heaving for several minutes in front of the entire Thanksgiving entourage. Even before the end of the day, Robby admitted to putting potato chips in the egg. So he revels in the fact that he was the instigator of the subterfuge.

Secondly, there is no reason why I would have manufactured the memory of Robby's unfortunate loss of his front teeth, as it wasn't traumatic for me. So as a matter of deduction, it is obvious I can see the future.

Learning

I was never a model student. In fact, I was a terrible one to begin with. I was in third grade when things began to change for me in this arena. I didn't know how to study, or specifically how to learn, at this point in my life. And being one of five children by the time I made it to third grade, my parents didn't have the time to participate too heavily in my studies. Helicopter parenting didn't exist back in the early 1970s, at least not at our house, so I was left to my own devices to take advantage of my educational opportunities. Third grade represented what I considered to be the real beginning of my education, as kindergarten, first, and second grades were brimming with coloring, recess, nap time, and lunch. I'm sure we did other things, but I was too young to recognize how teachers are masters of misdirection. Somehow, I learned the alphabet, to write my name, count to one hundred, and the difference between about twenty colors by the time I started third grade in Mrs. Estes's class.

My first report card from third grade showed Cs across the board in science, reading, and math. I know why my grades weren't stellar, but given my analytic strategy at the time, the fact I made Cs and not Fs was a miracle. All my tests at the time were multiple choice, and I used my visual acuity to answer the questions rather than any sort of cognitive insight. Basically, I used my thumb and index finger to compare the size of the potential answers with the blank space allotted for each answer. If the potential answer *fit* in the blank space, that was my answer. Needless to say, I was wrong pretty often. Again, getting a C using this method is pretty amazing. I think the teachers may have inadvertently assisted in my *success* using this method by accidentally leading me to better-than-expected results with blank spaces that actually did align with the physical size of most correct answers.

That first third-grade report card motivated me to shift my approach, and I actually began to get much better grades from that point on. The next couple of years of report cards show a steady stream of As and Bs. Something clicked in me about this time that still exists today—a desire to learn. Sometimes I'm a bit too in the weeds for the learning to have any real-world application, but there is satisfaction in small wins. For example, I was so proud of having learned my multiplication tables at this juncture of my learning experience that I expressed my favorite equation to my third-grade teacher. For some reason, I told Mrs. Estes that seven times six was my favorite math problem, and I was able to easily answer "Forty-two" when she asked me the answer. Then she quizzed me "What is six times seven?" Well, I was stumped. To this day, I know the answer to both these math problems, but when writing this anecdote, I had to use a calculator to confirm the answers continue to be forty-two.

Poker Face

From the time I was about five until I turned twelve, we lived in a small house on South Bamby Lane in Atlanta. One summer afternoon, when I was about eight or nine, I was playing alone (surprise) on the side of the house. I had come across some matches in the house earlier that day and decided to try them out without the prying eyes of anyone wanting to annex my experiment. I was able to strike a match and throw it into a small pile of pine straw next to our house. Much to my surprise (and excitement), it ignited, and the flames took over my little pile of straw very quickly. At precisely the time the straw ignited, my mother called to let me know that lunch was ready. I didn't know how to extinguish the fire, so I thought it would be best to just cover it up with more pine straw and go in for lunch. Remember the story about the fire truck? I guess being a juvenile arsonist isn't something that predisposes one to become a firefighter.

About three minutes after Mom, Michele, Chris, Robby, and I sat down to eat, our neighbor knocked on the back door and asked if there was a reason why there was a small fire on the side of our house. Everyone immediately raced outside to investigate the claim. I didn't need to see it since I already knew what the flames looked like, so I sat there and continued to eat my grilled cheese sandwich and tomato soup. Yes, I remember what I was eating to this day.

When everyone came back in the house after extinguishing the blaze, for some reason, everyone assumed I was the culprit. I just sat there eating my lunch and with my best poker face said I didn't know what they were talking about. I have always been easy to read whenever I did something wrong. I guess the next time I try to burn down the house, I'll run outside with everyone else and ask who in the world would do such a thing. That should help with my sociopathic tendencies.

Don't Go Up that Damn Hill

The front yard of our house on South Bamby Lane was three levels and not terribly conducive to riding bicycles. Luckily, our backyard was connected to the aforementioned cul-de-sac (the "turnaround"). The turnaround was at the end of a very short private drive that ran behind four houses (ours included), so we didn't have to worry about unfamiliar traffic whenever we were playing. This allowed us the opportunity to play without Mom and Dad being afraid we would be run over by someone racing through the neighborhood (that happened in the street in the front yard).

The turnaround was an oblong paved circle with a small patch of grass in the center that stood in as our baseball and football fields. There were two very distinct *corners* to manage whenever we ran, rode our bicycles, or, of course, drove our Gremlin go-cart. One corner was a patch of gravel that never seemed to go away despite how often we tried to shovel or sweep it up. The other challenge corner was an area covered with sand about three or four inches deep at its deepest, and about ten feet long. Again, a natural hazard that was impossible to remove despite how often we tried.

Now the entrance to the turnaround was at the top of a mountain (to an eight-year-old child)… Actually, the acme of this hill was probably about fifteen feet above the main part of the cul-de-sac. This incline offered lots of excitement to us, and we used it often to get some speed on our bicycles to begin the jaunt around the turnaround. Unfortunately, Mom constantly demanded, "Don't go up that hill. You'll get hurt!" and we were reprimanded anytime she found we were doing so, especially with our bikes.

One day, Robby and I were outside riding bicycles, and I decided it was a great time to test out the new (to me) three-speed bicycle Dad had recently purchased for me at a local police auction for something like $3. It was a handsome bike despite being secondhand, as it was a beautiful midnight blue and had a back tire that resembled a super-adhesive dragster slick. Similar to many other bikes in the 1970s, this bike had the requisite banana seat to make riding comfortable for hours at a time.

Despite the constant warnings from my mother, I walked the bicycle to the top of the hill and prepared myself to race down the hill and slam on the brakes in the gravel trap at the bottom like I had done hundreds of times before on my old bicycle (don't tell my mom about my many previous times up and down the damn hill). Well, after two or three quick acceleration pedals, I picked up sufficient speed to allow me to make a big dustup when I stopped right in front of Robby as he waited for his turn to take on the hill. I had never taken a class in bicycle riding, and as such, was not prepared for any emergency that might arise, like, say, the loss of braking power when the chain dislodged from the gears. Incidentally, it seems strange that a major bicycle company wouldn't install redundant braking systems to protect children who disobeyed their parents and rode too fast without sufficient time to allow for orderly (and SAFE) stopping operations. And who in the world would engineer a cul-de-sac without a proper breakdown lane? Now that I think about it, I probably should have sued the bicycle company, the police auction, and/or the builder of the house for allowing this to happen. I'm sure I would win a lawsuit, but the statute of limitations has likely expired.

Nonetheless, as you can surmise from the previous statements, about halfway down the damn hill, the chain came off the gears resulting in exponentially increasing velocity until I arrived at the approximate speed of sound. And without the luxury of brakes, the only thing I could think to do was drag my feet (actually it was the toes of my shoes, as my feet didn't easily reach the ground on this "big boy's bike") to try and slow my arrival in the gravel trap. Oh, and I failed to mention that about ten feet past the gravel trap was a perpetual sticker bush that had consumed many baseballs over the years. So my goal was to avoid the sticker landing pad as the toes of my tennis shoes began to melt from the two-hundred-degree temperature of the friction between the rubber and asphalt.

The smell of the rubber on my shoes disintegrating is as fresh to me today as it was then. This approach wasn't working, so I had to come up with an alternative to hitting the sticker bush and ending up looking like Pinhead from the Hellraiser movie franchise for the rest of my life. So I decided to ditch the bike and try to absorb the impact by rolling to a stop on my own. Another approach that didn't work out so well. When I tried to lean to one side, the handlebars abruptly jolted to the left and I flew over them face-first into the dreaded gravel trap.

Robby's point of view of this accident obviously was very different from mine. For me, it was terrifying, and I was crying as the dust settled while Robby was laughing. I managed to muster the strength to get myself out of the mangled mess of gravel, melted tennis shoes, crashed bicycle parts, and blood up to the house where our Great-Aunt Bebo (our constant babysitter in those days) immediately attended to my physical wounds. Upon seeing my injuries, Bebo summoned my mother from her job as a shoe distributor for Butler's Shoes to come home to thoroughly attend to my injuries. Bebo's medical triaging skills were limited, but she noticed some blood on one of my arms and thought it would be good to secure my arm to make sure it didn't fall off while we waited for Mom to arrive. So she used an old cloth diaper (I think it was a clean one) as a sling, and it paid off by keeping my arm attached to my torso for fifteen to twenty minutes before Mom pulled into the driveway.

When Mom arrived, she immediately screamed, "What the hell happened?"

I think I was clear in my explanation, but I suspect all I was able to get out was, "Blubby, Robby, bloo, blah, laughed at me, wahhh." In what you might surmise as something akin to my mother's intuition, Mom determined I was hurt, and my needs exceeded her capacity to heal. After all, rubbing alcohol, Band-Aids, and hugs were not going to make these injuries go away. So we were off to secure professional assistance from our family doctor just a few miles from our home.

Dr. Watkins received me into his exam room and proceeded to determine that I was suffering from several minor injuries that rubbing alcohol, Band-Aids, and a short regiment of hugs would probably heal. However, there was one that required a more skillful hand. It seems that when I went over the handlebars, my face and arm weren't the only things that took a direct hit. The index finger on my right hand hit the ground with such force that the nail was 90 percent dislodged from the finger (held by a small piece of skin at the first knuckle). So Dr. Watkins skillfully removed the cigarette from his mouth, coughed a couple of times, and then took a pair of what I hope were sterilized surgical scissors and proceeded to completely remove the nail. It was traumatic for both me and Mom, but I was the one left with a permanent physical deformity from how much skin was removed from my finger during that surgical procedure. The nail grew back, but the loss of about one-quarter of an inch of skin in the center of my finger has resulted in a nail that has a convex "V"-shaped ridge to it. I'm embarrassed to have people notice this to this day, but I've become pretty good at keeping it out of view.

On the way back home from the doctor's office, Mom, now calmed from all the excitement, said, "I told you not to go up that damn hill. I told you, you would get hurt!" I explained to Mom that going up the hill was fine; it was coming down that actually caused the problem. She didn't appreciate my clarification of events, and I lost privileges to my bicycle. Interesting punishment, as it was just a heap of awkwardly bent metal now, and there was *no way* I was going to get on a bike again that didn't have redundant braking systems.

CHAPTER 7

Learning Along the Way

God-given talent

After Tracey and I were married for about a year, her parents decided to take the family to Park City, Utah, for a ski vacation. I had never been snow skiing and had no idea of the difference between a ski bib and bindings. So this was going to be an adventure for me, one that I leaned into a bit just to get as much out of the experience as I could.

Tracey's father was a frequent flyer and had tons of airline points he could use to fly us first class from Fort Lauderdale. As we were sipping on champagne (it was probably Coke, but I like to think I took full advantage of first class), I casually told Tracey I was a natural at snow skiing. After about two minutes of snickering (and maybe a disdainful side-eyed stare), Tracey was able to muster the question, "How do you figure?" My response caused her to laugh even harder and longer than she did from my original protestation. I explained that God gives everyone a talent, and snow skiing is mine because I've tried everything else. Interestingly enough, I did pick it up pretty quickly and, after the first two times accidentally finding myself going down the slopes backward, I was able to master this particular skill and impress most of the middle-aged first-timers. So even some-one in their late twenties can learn a new skill. I just learned how to replicate an accidental occurrence and parlay it into a completely useless skill. I like to think I look cool doing something that almost no one else does. It did come in handy many years later when I took Nicholas on his first skiing trip with his Boy Scout troop. By assisting Nicholas in his first few runs, facing him, and giving him pointers as we descended the slopes, I impressed Nicholas's Boy Scout colleagues and a couple of their parents with my obvious athleticism and agility.

Eclectically Average

Looking back on my life, I think the approach that best describes my style closely resembles a liberal arts education. Dad used to say he was a *jack-of-all-trades and master of none.* Well, I kind of feel that way about myself. I've tried lots of things in my life, and I seem to pick up the basics of all of them pretty easily. The problem is I also get bored very easily. So once I understand the basics, I tend to move on to the next thing.

For example, I received an electric guitar when I was twelve years old as a consolation gift from my parents for making me move to a new school just before my seventh-grade year. The reason this was a consolation gift is that, at the end of my sixth-grade year at Skyland Elementary School, I was chosen to be a Safety Patrol Crossing Guard for the following year. At the end of each school year, all the students who performed as Safety Patrol Guards were allowed to take a trip to Washington, D.C., as a reward. Robby was able to do this the year before, and I was looking forward to my chance to take the train ride to our nation's capital myself. Well, our move to Duluth upended that opportunity. So my parents' guilt landed in my lap in the form of a shiny new black lacquer 1974 Univox guitar with a white pickguard. Along with the guitar came several weeks of lessons. Cut to the chase here: I've been playing this same guitar for more than forty-five years, and the only thing I've mastered is "Smoke on the Water" by Deep Purple…well, and much to the disdain of my children, I am getting pretty good at Jack White's "Seven Nation Army" and "Cake by the Ocean" by DNCE.

A slightly modified mark to Dad's *jack-of-all-trades* moniker, I proudly self-identify as *eclectically average* or *averagely eclectic*. I say this because, as I've mentioned before, I have tried a great deal of things in my life and find myself being able to do most things at a level easily defined as *sufficient*. My career experiences have run the gamut from bagging groceries to selling boats and motorhomes to being an "Ace Helpful Hardware Man." Most people I know are surprised to learn I was also a meat cutter (butcher's apprentice) and an air traffic controller before I settled on my thirty-plus-year career in public health. And as mentioned above, I would consider my skills in all these areas satisfactory. However, to the obvious benefit of the flying public, I decided that being "good enough" was probably not the performance level considered appropriate for an air traffic controller, and I moved on to other endeavors.

Chicken Fingers

When I was fifteen, I began working to earn money to purchase my first car. The first job I took was at a fast-food restaurant called Granny's Fried Chicken in Duluth, Georgia. I lasted one eight-hour shift and decided to retire from my culinary career when I realized

I was not cut out for this line of work. I learned three things during my tenure at Granny's:

(1) Whenever you finished frying the chicken, you were to dump it into the triage bin and loudly exclaim, "Granny's fresh fried chicken is up!"

(2) The secret to Granny's fried chicken was more in the brine solution than in the batter mixture. I don't think Granny's is still in business, but I'm likely still bound by the non-disclosure agreement preventing me from disclosing the secret brine ingredients. So Granny's executives and lawyers: Your secret will remain hidden from the world for the time being; and

(3) Even your fingers can look good when they're fried to golden brown crispy perfection. They don't taste as good as Granny's fresh fried chicken, but they sure look nice.

My first and only day at Granny's was spent learning how to marinate chicken in the famous (albeit furtive) brine solution and, most specifically, how to make sure the chicken legs didn't have the skin fall down to their ankles during the frying process. It wasn't that the work was mind-numbing (it was) that made me rethink my employment options; it was that I found the five-hundred-degree grease to be too big a risk for my tender teenage hands.

You see, there is a clever way to make sure the skin on the chicken legs doesn't fall down like loose socks when you're frying them. If you simply bread them and drop them into the fryer, the skin will bundle at the ankle, and you'll end up with a not-so-appealing chicken leg with most of the meat uncovered and the skin at the ankle like a pair of socks with worn-out elastic bindings. So to prevent this from happening, you must remove the chicken legs from the brine solution by grabbing the ankle with one hand and rolling the skin down (or up, as it were) to completely cover the meaty part of the leg. Then you hand-bread each leg by rolling them in the batter mixture. This process results in complete coverage of your hands in the batter mixture, as this was well before fast-food restaurants were using latex gloves.

The last step is to hold the legs by the ankle between your thumb and index fingers and slowly submerge the meaty part of the leg just long enough to begin to fry the skin in place (about three seconds) before dropping them into the grease.

Well, after submerging my hands in the icy brine solution and breading a couple of dozen chicken legs, my hands were pretty numb. I then began grabbing the legs two at a time and doing the dance, counting to three each time before dropping the legs and repeating the process until all were in the fryer. What I didn't realize was that my fingers, while not actually being submerged in the grease, were close enough to fry the batter mixture that had caked onto my hands into a beautiful golden brown masterpiece. From the middle knuckle on, the index and middle fingers of both hands resembled the crust of a fully cooked piece of chicken. I think this is where the term *chicken fingers* came from. Surprisingly, deep-frying your fingers isn't all that painful, as my index and middle fingers on both hands were only tender for a few days after the incident. But it was sufficiently impactful that I turned in my polyester uniform the very next day.

When All Else Fails, Sweep

After the harrowing experience at Granny's, I mustered up the courage to find another job, this time steering away from boiling vats of grease to find something a little less scar-inducing. I was able to secure a position at a family-owned grocery store in Duluth, Georgia, called Parson's. While most high school employees at Parson's were bagging groceries in the front of the store, I was hired to work in the produce department in the back. I arrived after school every afternoon around three o'clock and worked until the store closed at six. The produce manager at Parson's was a generally friendly fellow named Frank. I think he had been with the store for about one hundred years, but it's likely he was only about sixty when I met him. I think Frank may well have been the inspiration for the character Eustace Bagge from *Courage the Cowardly Dog*, as he is the spitting image of Frank (at least in my memory). Each day before he left at four o'clock, Frank would write a list of tasks for me to complete before the store closed. Frank was pretty good at estimating how long my list needed to be so I wouldn't run out of things to do by the end of the day. Being fifteen years old, having this kind of structure was great, as it kept me focused and away from my natural tendency to get bored.

After about a year of my produce department gig at Parson's, the family decided to close the store to expand its department store footprint. I was once again looking for an after-school job. It didn't take long for me to find a job at another grocery store, as my experience in the produce department was in high demand. So I started working at a new store in Stone Mountain called Big Apple Food Warehouse. This was a great move for me, mainly because I commanded a higher hourly wage from a big corporate grocery store chain and I worked more hours. I usually arrived at the Big Apple around four o'clock and worked until the store closed at ten. The main difference in the work was that there was no "Eustace" (Frank) there to provide me with a list of things to do for my entire shift. I usually overlapped my time with an assistant manager, and he left me with a verbal list of major things to accomplish. Needless to say, I struggled with this lack of structure and found myself getting bored within the first couple of months.

Finally, my guilty conscience began to take control, and I was feeling increasingly uncomfortable with getting paid for six hours a night to do about three hours of work. The rest of my shift was spent walking around and straightening things. So one night, I approached the store manager to have him tell me what I needed to do. The manager (Mr. Davis) politely gave me a few things to do that first night, and I finally felt like I earned my salary. This happened a few more times before Don's patient and measured demeanor took an unexpected turn. It was clear he was a bit goaded by my constant need for direction, and he walked me to a quiet spot on the floor in the produce department for a private conversation. What he said to me that day has stuck with me all these years, and I think it gave me something that many people don't learn until well into adulthood. Mr. Davis said, "We don't only pay you to do things. We actually pay you to think too! Your job is to take care of the produce department and attend to customer needs. Use your brain and figure out for yourself what needs to be done in order to make us successful." Then he added this one last bit of advice: "When all else fails, sweep."

It was at that moment that I realized I had more to offer an employer than just some robotic existence to simply do a simple set of predetermined tasks; I could actually use my brain to help the business in ways not initially considered when I was hired. I have taken this approach to every other job since Big Apple, including in my career with the CDC. I've recounted this story to many folks over the years, and it seems to have similar results with folks struggling with how to contribute to a larger organization within the confines of their position. I remind them the goal is not to simply check off boxes but to look for ways to make the organization better, even if it isn't within the boundaries of their position description. And I remind them that if they can't identify something new and innovative, get back to the basics, and "when all else fails, sweep."

Mobile Marketing

I once answered a job advertisement in *The Atlanta Journal-Constitution* for a "marketing" position with the hopes I could find a more white-collar career. It was in my senior year of high school when I was in between grocery store jobs and desperate to find a way to make money for my car payment. I didn't have the luxury of working for Dad at the time, as he was straddling his entrepreneurial opportunities at this particular time as well. However, he was happy to encourage me to test the waters of this *high-brow* marketing job. I think he knew what this was all about, but he never let on that someone with more discerning skills might find this opportunity to be a little on the shady side.

I was pleasantly surprised to be immediately offered an in-person interview when I called the number in the ad. My impeccable experiences at Granny's, Parson's, and Big Apple obviously impressed the owner of the company. I arrived at the interview dressed as suggested (in comfortable shoes and loose-fitting clothes). Being just sixteen years old, nothing about this raised a red flag at all. What I learned was this wasn't so much an interview as it was an audition to see how successful I might be in selling miscellaneous electronic items (interestingly new, in-the-box items with the stickers from local retail establishments still affixed) out of the trunk of a car in the middle of downtown Atlanta. I was paired with an associate (strangely the *owner* of the company), and I found the loose-fitting clothes and comfortable shoes came in handy when we needed to relocate the sales floor (the spacious trunk of a 1974 Chevrolet Caprice) to another location rather swiftly. Surprisingly, we were able to offload most of the merchandise for the day, and we split the profits right there on the spot. I think my take for the day was in the neighborhood of thirty dollars…all untaxed, mind you. So I hope there aren't any IRS agents reading this and feeling the need to have me make amends for my one day on the job without paying taxes in 1981. I probably failed to pay about $4 in taxes, but with interest and fines, it'd likely be approaching six figures by now.

Home Invasion

As mentioned earlier, Tracey and I moved to Fort Lauderdale shortly after we were married so I could begin my public health career with the CDC. We rented a small apartment on the second floor overlooking the apartment complex pool in Plantation (about five miles from downtown Fort Lauderdale and about thirty miles from Miami). I was an avid watcher of the TV series *Miami Vice* and was conditioned to believe that drug dealing and prostitution were rampant all over Miami (and by extension, Fort Lauderdale). I admit that I never witnessed a car chase with a Ferrari-driving undercover police officer, but the crime I saw on the nightly news made me believe we lived all too close to a thriving bevy of criminals.

Our apartment wasn't much, but we thought it was nice and we proceeded to cram as much stuff into the seven hundred square feet as possible. Most of our worldly belongings at the time consisted of kitchenware (mostly wedding gifts) and clothes. The kitchen was small, and we didn't have space to store all the appliances in cabinets or the small pantry (which, by the way, shared space with our washer and dryer). So we stored a good number of kitchen items on the shelf of our bedroom closet. And since this apartment housed all our worldly possessions, we were keen to keep the apartment door locked at all times to protect us from having to deal with known criminal elements that were always on the run from Detectives Crockett and Tubbs.

One night around three in the morning, Tracey and I were awakened by a loud bang, alerting us to a possible intruder in the apartment. I didn't have access to any weapons, and my golf clubs were out on our deck on the other side of the apartment. And being a newlywed, I felt responsible to protect our belongings (oh yeah, and Tracey too) from any harm. So I got out of bed very cautiously and scanned the room to make sure the intruder hadn't yet made their way into the bedroom. To my great horror, I heard a shuffling noise coming from the closet across the room. This was the most afraid I had been in my life to this point, but I was determined to face the criminal(s) rummaging through the thousands of dollars in blenders, toasters, and spatulas in the closet. So I inched my way toward the closet door while audibly moaning in fear.

Upon arriving at the closet door less than a minute after being awakened by the loud crashing noise, I reached for the closet door knob and yanked it open to confront the culprit and hopefully surprise them so much that they didn't have time to shoot or stab me before I could wrestle them out the front door of the apartment. To my great surprise, the closet door only partially opened because several of our worldly possessions had proven to be too much for the shelf to handle and had fallen when the shelf separated from the wall…no sign of anyone there to shatter the illusion of safety in our apartment.

All the excitement that night was because we put a heavy blender, mixer, and toaster on a closet shelf that was rated for maybe just a single toaster. I'm not sure I learned anything more from this experience than to make sure not to overload a closet shelf, but I suspect that I'm now less likely to base my fears on dangers or stereotypes perpetuated in 1980s television series.

Public Health in Action

My first job after Tracey and I were married was with the Centers for Disease Control (and Prevention was added in 1992) as a public health associate/advisor with the Division of Sexually Transmitted Diseases. My first assignment was in Fort Lauderdale doing frontline public health work counseling patients on the hazards of sexually transmitted diseases (including HIV/AIDS), interviewing those with positive tests for these diseases to ascertain their sexual partners, and locating these partners to have them tested and treated. As you might imagine, I have plenty of stories related to my early career. Many of these aren't suitable for retelling to a sensitive audience, so the adults reading this book should be on the lookout for my next book, *What the Hell Is Condylomata Lata? More Family Secrets.*

Working in South Florida, it is commonplace to interact with others whose first language is not English. So as part of our training, we were instructed to have referral letters pre-written in Spanish and Creole, instructing those who have come into contact with a person with a positive STD test to seek medical attention at a health care facility. I am not at all fluent in Spanish, but I did take a couple of years of Spanish in high school, thereby allowing me only a strong appreciation for the differences between the Spanish and English languages. One day, I was tasked with finding a person for testing with a name that led me to believe he was Hispanic. On the chance we would not be able to communicate when I found him, I took a pre-written referral letter with me with his name on the outside of a sealed envelope.

After doing some investigation, I was able to locate this person's address. I'll call him "John" to maintain his confidentiality. When I arrived at his house, a woman appeared at the door. She explained she didn't speak English, so I reached way back to high school and asked, "*¿Es esta la casa de Juan?*" When she confirmed that John lived there, I held up the letter and said very slowly and loudly, "*Give him this letter.*" I had impressed myself with being able to ask if John lived there, but since I didn't need to know where the bathroom was or to tell her that my pencil was yellow, I was completely out of the relationally functional Spanish I'd learned in (or retained from) high school. She had a confused look on her face when she took the letter, but all turned out well for everyone. John came into the clinic the next day and received a clean bill of health. So the nice lady who politely didn't laugh at my troubled attempt to communicate somehow understood what I was trying to say.

Looking back on this experience and comparing it to the time in elementary school when I exclaimed I had met someone who "spoke in cursive," it isn't nearly as endearing when a twenty-six-year-old displays this sort of ignorance. It was successful, but nonetheless ignorant.

Travel

As a child, and reminding you my family consisted of four (ultimately five) children and two parents living in a small two-bedroom, one-bath house, we didn't have a lot of money to travel very often. We did occasionally drive up to Columbia, South Carolina, to visit distant relatives and take vacations down in Florida. Despite my exceptional ability to remember back to when I was around three years old, I do not recall anything about our family's move across the country when I was about one. The stories I've heard about the reasoning for our cross-country relocation center around Dad wanting to get away and try something completely new…oh, and there was something about him being told many times he could be a movie star or something like that. So for whatever reason, my parents decided to take four children (ages ranging from one to six) on a road trip from Georgia to California to start a new chapter in our lives. This was a short-lived chapter, as I believe we moved back to Georgia after having spent about a year with Dad making a living as a pool shark…yes, a pool shark. I guess there were only so many suckers in

Camarillo, California, from which to win money, so we had to come back home for better career prospects.

Again, I have absolutely no recollection of what traveling across the country and back in a two-door automobile (without air conditioning) with five other human beings was like. I suspect it was terribly uncomfortable and equally boring for all the other humans. I wonder if this was my implanted "alien" family or my real family. If it was the aliens trying to gauge how I would react to the situation, obviously they had no clue that stimuli for a one-year-old human didn't expand much past the need for food and a clean diaper. Needless to say, I don't think this trip either piqued or stunted my interest in travel. Nor did it provide the otherworldly observers any useful information to relay back to the mothership.

My parents had an affinity for Daytona Beach, Florida, as a vacation spot. So I have lots of memories of times we went to the "World's Most Famous Beach." The two that come to mind are connected to learning to swim and understanding the absolute imperative of sunscreen (we called it suntan lotion at the time).

My father was a good swimmer, and he enjoyed an abundance of melanin pigmentation. That is, he was well-tanned year-round and could stay in the sun for hours without fear of getting sunburned. In fact, Dad's condition usually resulted in his skin darkening during the summer months to the point that people sometimes mistook him for having some Native American or African ancestry. The bottom line here is that Dad never suffered from sunburn.

On one trip to Daytona when I was about five, I was in the hotel pool (again, five years old…still afraid of the ocean) learning to swim by sitting on an inflatable pool float. As I was drifting into the deep end, my father dove in and pulled the float out from under me. I quickly ingested about seven gallons of water and died for about five minutes. Well, that's a slight exaggeration. I took on a mouthful of pool water when I went under and then cried for about five minutes, telling everyone in the pool area that my father tried to kill me. His reasoning for doing this was to introduce me to the literal *immersion model* of learning. Ultimately, I don't think I learned to swim that day, but I sure learned how to flail. And I guess this taught me not to try and breathe underwater. Another lesson learned…thanks, Dad!

My mother is the exact opposite of my father in the melanin pigmentation game. She is very fair-skinned and burns reasonably easily. I also lost the melanin pigmentation lottery and do not tolerate the ultraviolet light offered by the sun very well. The trip to Daytona mentioned above is where I was pragmatically diagnosed with this deficiency. This trip was three or four days, and on the first day, we stayed outside on the beach or at the pool for most of the afternoon. My brother Robby shares the tanning traits of my father more so than of Mom, so spending the same amount of time outside that day resulted in two different outcomes…Robby tanned nicely, and I ended up with blisters on my shoulders. The blisters were about one-quarter inch high and extremely painful. The second and third days of this trip were spent with us trying to figure out how to reduce the pain and avoid additional damage while spending more time outside with everyone else in the family. Dad's solution was for me to wear a T-shirt when I got in the pool so the sun wouldn't make the blisters worse. It's hard to tell if wearing a T-shirt actually helped avoid third-degree burns on top of the base second-degree burns, but I can tell you this: it hurts like hell to remove a wet T-shirt from fresh blisters on your shoulders. I still have the physical scars from these blisters to this day. So now I wear long-sleeve shirts that repel ultraviolet rays whenever I'm outside for any amount of time, and I always try to sit in the shade to avoid repeating this lesson.

I'm not sure if it was actually the lack of resources or a lack of desire to see other places that dominated my parents' reluctance to travel, but it doesn't really matter. The result was they didn't travel very often (or far) for most of their lives. Neither one had ever been to another country until they were in their forties. Dad had technically been out of the country a few times when he went deep-sea fishing, but you don't tend to interact with other cultures, sightsee at UNESCO World Heritage sites, or speak a different language when you're just twelve miles off the coast of the United States. I often joke that my father's impressions of locales outside what he was familiar with were, like mine, built on what he saw on TV. For example, traveling to New York City meant you had to protect yourself from the elements presented on *Kojak*. And Northern California was dangerous because of what he had seen on *The Streets of San Francisco*. Dad never traveled to either of these places, but he was quick to warn us of the dangers before one of his children decided to risk certain robberies and death to see a new place.

Who Loves You, Baby?

I began getting the bug to travel about the time I graduated from high school. Immediately upon graduating, I moved to Daytona Beach, Florida, to start my flight training at Embry-Riddle Aeronautical University. Going to Embry-Riddle offered me the opportunity to meet people from around the world and hear first-hand about many intriguing places. My first roommate was from Japan, and there were so many other students from around the world that I couldn't help but be inspired to see all the places I heard about from my classmates. I still haven't been to Japan, but I will get there one day, and I hope to catch up with Yoshio.

My wanderlust was conceived at Embry-Riddle, and the first time I had the chance to take advantage of a trip out of my comfort zone was when a friend from high school, Mark Adams, invited me to go to the land of Telly Savalas' *Kojak* (NYC) in 1986. Dad's advice before we left for the airport was to carry most of our money in our shoes so we'd still have cash after we were inevitably mugged and/or pickpocketed. He further suggested we walk with a purpose even if we didn't know where we were going and to absolutely never look up at the top of the buildings—all of this in service of keeping us from looking like tourists. We never got mugged or pickpocketed, which is a good thing because both Mark and I had forgotten to hide any cash in our shoes.

To this day, I still can't figure out how not to look like a tourist in New York City when you're lugging your suitcases across the city to get to your hotel. I'll admit I tried to keep my eyes looking more toward the ground than the top of the buildings, but I suspect my southern accent betrayed my faux Brooklyn upbringing.

Go West, Young Man

That same year, I embarked on another trip that will undoubtedly remain in my memory for the rest of my life. A longtime friend of the family had just returned to Georgia after having moved to Los Angeles for a year or two. Bill Patton was a professional singer here in Georgia, so he wanted to give this a go in the entertainment capital of the world. After giving this his best shot, Bill decided it was time to pack up and move back to Georgia to resume a career outside of Hollywood. He still had his apartment in LA but needed to make a trip out to pack all his belongings before returning to Georgia for good. So Bill and I decided to make the trip together and make it a three-week vacation.

I don't recall any fatherly advice for this trip, as I was doing this one with a great family friend who was a little older than me and had lived on the West Coast for a while. That trip stoked my desire to travel in so many ways, and I am very fortunate to have so many good memories, mostly because Bill was a great guide and his curiosity led us to a lot of great experiences. We were able to see nearly the entire state. We flew into San Francisco, drove through Napa Valley and Muir Woods, and on up to Eureka. From there, we drove down the Pacific Coast Highway all the way to Los Angeles.

The big memories from this trip were driving through a giant redwood tree, seeing the most beautiful craggy coastline from Monterey to Santa Barbara, meeting several actors and entertainers, and being thrown off the set of *Invaders from Mars* because we ate from the catering table. It was Bill's Dagwood-sized sandwich that garnered all the unwanted attention, as I was only eating some Cheetos and drinking Sprite.

My First Appearance on National Television

It was on this trip to LA that I came to sing on *The Tonight Show*. I did mention that Bill was a professional singer at the time, and he and I were honored to sing for Johnny Carson on this nationally broadcast program. This is generally how I introduce the situation to people, and after a little cajoling, despite my insistence that I have a video to prove it (which I do), I give up the full story. But I don't open up before I get enough attention to feel some degree of celebrity.

The short (and more accurate) story is that Bill and I decided to go to a taping of *The Tonight Show*, and we were in the audience on the rare occasion they did a bit of encouraging the audience to sing made-up lyrics. Well, Bill and I happened to be in the right place at the right time to be on screen several times for a cumulative total of about five seconds. So that's how I came to sing on *The Tonight Show* with Johnny Carson. And by the way, residuals for this don't pay as well as you might think.

Oh, and the final memory from that trip was when we drove to Las Vegas for a few days, where I won enough on a slot machine that weekend to pay for my entire three-week vacation. I've since lost three times that much in subsequent visits to Sin City.

Domestic Travel

Since taking my job with the CDC, I've traveled a great deal domestically. While I haven't been to all fifty states yet, I've made a significant dent at the expense of US taxpayers. In each instance, I try to do something interesting in my off hours that I can't do at home. I've been fortunate to take in a game at (old) Yankee Stadium with two coworkers, see bison lounging by a river in North Dakota with snow bonding to their huge manes, watch the Lakers play the Suns in Phoenix (unfortunately sans Kobe Bryant, as he was injured and couldn't make the trip), and spend time at the Art Institute of Chicago seeing firsthand some of the most famous works of art in

America. I've also had the best brisket in the world in Kansas City and a $38 grilled cheese sandwich in New York City.

While these are great memories, I still want to go back to nearly all of the places I've traveled for work in order to really get to know these places (and the people) without the burden of having to work during the day and squeeze out more satisfying experiences each evening. Unfortunately, it'll have to be without the assistance of the hard-working, taxpaying citizens of the United States.

My Name Is Birama Traore

My first working international trip with the CDC involved traveling to the West African nation of Mali in late February/early March of 2001. I was tapped to write a computer program for a small HIV clinic in Bamako and then travel there to install it, train the employees on how to use it, and observe its use in a real-world setting for a few days. I was there for two weeks, and absolutely everything about this trip was life-changing for me. First, I had only been away from home once for more than about a week (the California trip mentioned above). Second, traveling internationally was still novel to me, as I had only been to Mexico once before this trip across the ocean. And being in a place where I was at a huge communication disadvantage put me in a new and vulnerable position. I was blown away by how warm, accepting, and loving everyone was. I never felt uncomfortable, and I was made to feel like a resident of the community every moment I was there. I was told several times that Malians have a saying that "every man is a poor man," meaning we all have a moral responsibility to help others regardless of what it looks like they have.

Eid al-Adha (also known as Tabaski) happened to fall during my first visit to Mali. Tabaski is celebrated throughout the Muslim world as a commemoration of Prophet Abraham's willingness to sacrifice everything for God. This four-day Islamic festival begins with sunrise prayers at the local mosque and involves families coming together for several days to prepare to slaughter a ram in a ritual sacrifice. It was explained to me as something akin to Thanksgiving in the US (obviously with more religious connotations). Several colleagues and I were invited to a local family's Tabaski celebration to visit with their extended family and dine on the family's prized goat on the last day of the holiday (Tuesday, March 6, 2001). As the men took care of cooking the goat in an outdoor fire pit, the women remained busy in the kitchen preparing all the accoutrements for our meal. This left all the children to prepare for their visit to the mosque later in the day by cycling through their haute couture in a sort of fashion show for their foreign visitors. I felt like part of the family that day (the entire day), and watching the children (ages about three to fourteen) own the runway was the highlight of the day.

The patriarch of the family was about my age, and neither of us spoke the other's language enough to converse at any deep level. During the course of the day, our host confessed that my name was difficult for him to pronounce. So his remedy for this challenge was to give me a Malian name that would be easier to roll off his tongue. He decided I would from this point on be known as Birama Traore. Not only was I excited to have a new Malian name, but I was extremely honored to learn that this was the name of his best friend from primary school.

Truth be told, I am a little torn between the fashion show and the honor of receiving a name that was obviously very prized by our host as being my favorite part of the day. However, there was one additional honor bestowed upon us during the Tabaski celebration. As valued guests in the home, we were offered the most prized part of the goat. I knew it was considered bad manners to turn down the delicacy of the meal from the host, but I just couldn't see myself being able to consume the head of a grilled goat. Besides, I thought it would be best if I only offended them with rejection and didn't further insult them by requiring them to clean up after what can only be described as a 100 percent chance of retching. Besides, vomit might have sullied the honor of my new name.

The weekend I was in the country was spent on a short jaunt (about 400 miles from Bamako) to Mopti and Bandiagara in central Mali. We left mid-day on Friday and drove for about eight hours to our accommodations in Mopti. The majority of the trip was uneventful, if not terribly bumpy. There was one instance when we came across several fifty-five-gallon metal drums with open flames strategically positioned across the road, fashioning a makeshift toll booth. It was dark when we came across this road hazard, and the glow of the fires emanating from the drums masked the three or four young men just off the side of the road awaiting their prey. Our driver, Abdraman, had experienced this sort of ruse before and was having none of it whatsoever. He commenced negotiating/arguing with the swindlers and after about five minutes, and the exponential increase of stress on the faces of the foreign passengers in the car, Abdraman relinquished a 500 CFA note to gain passage from the nocturnal toll collectors. It was an uncomfortable situation, but for the price of about $1 in US currency, we were allowed to peaceably pass. Whew, I'm just glad this negotiation didn't end in someone feeling the need to urinate on us.

A little further on in our trip, we stopped on the side of the road to stretch and take a look at the night sky. I was astounded by how dark it was and how bright all the stars were. At one point, I saw a light moving across the sky that was way too high to be an airplane. I asked Abdraman if it was a shooting star. The answer was, "No, it's just a satellite." Coming from a country where light pollution is so pervasive, I never realized you could see a satellite with the naked eye. Our driver may have considered my naiveté endearing, but the look on his face was probably more contempt or sadness. He may have even mumbled under his breath something like, "Bless his little heart."

The remainder of the drive to Mopti was uneventful, and we took up residence at the Hôtel Kanaga. The hotel didn't provide much of an impression, as I do not recall even the basics of the room. We awoke on Saturday in Mopti and spent the morning at a market on the banks of the Niger River. I didn't buy anything, but I was fascinated with one of the main commodities being sold in the market…salt. Nearly all the vendors had tablets of salt in their booths and on their boats. It looked like blocks of cocaine wrapped in cellophane (remember my fascination with *Miami Vice*). So I took some photos to impress all my friends back home.

The trek to Bandiagara was incredibly bumpy, as the road along the route was apparently a footpath that was substantially gullied out by years of use by both human foot traffic and the occasional donkey-drawn buggy. Engineers had been working on a permanent road along the well-traveled route from Mopti to Bandiagara for some time, but alas, our trip was about three years ahead of completion. So all we could do was look longingly at the road being constructed alongside the path that would make this route much more comfortable and fast for future travelers.

We arrived in Bandiagara around noon and were immediately met by a group of ten to twelve children singing in a natural tunnel that serves as the trailhead for our hike down the escarpment. I'm sure welcoming foreign visitors to the cliffs of the Dogon people is something the locals have found to be pretty lucrative. Nonetheless, I was impressed with the overt attempt for our money and wrangled the children together for a group photo, for which I provided a nominal fee for the privilege.

Our hike down the cliffs was incredible. We hired a guide and were offered a master class on the history of the Dogon people and the structures used by these cliff-dwellers. We learned about the buildings, roughly the size of small storage sheds, used to store grain, where the families slept (mostly on the roofs because of the heat from the proximity of the Sahara Desert), and the buildings used for menstruation. All of the buildings are constructed from mud bricks, and those not intended for dwelling were topped with cone-shaped thatch roofs. Many of the structures were adorned with intricately carved window shutters and doors depicting either the purpose of the building or some mythological story. I was awed by the detail included in these carvings. I also found it interesting that tourists were offered these as tchotchkes (about half the size of the originals) that replicate many of the doors and window shutters seen along the way. While I found them to be beautiful, the size made them impractical for me to transport back home in my carry-on luggage.

In an hour and a half, we made it down to the bottom of the cliffs, where we were met by village elders and treated to lunch on the covered rooftop where the important business of the village is convened. We were served couscous with tomatoes and onions grown in the village. We passed by the onion fields on our way into the village at the top of the cliffs earlier in the day. As a result of the fastidious work of the women of the village transporting buckets of water from wells several miles away each day, these fields were a stark green contrast to the brown surroundings of this very arid region. At lunch, bread was served as well, and I later learned the crunchy part of the bread was sand accidentally mixed into the dough. As Bandiagara is on the edge of the Sahara Desert, the winds allow the sands to infiltrate just about everything. I was so hungry at the conclusion of the hike that sandy bread was a nonissue.

However, there was one issue that taught me a lesson that I keep to this day. The temperature approached 120 degrees the day we traversed the cliff. And being in a predominantly Muslim country, we were all instructed to respectfully wear long pants despite the stifling heat. Given the heat of the area and my jeans, I was also warned to drink lots of water to avoid dehydration. I took this to heart and consumed about two gallons that day without any pit stops to offload any of that water. By the time I retreated to my room for the night in the Campement Hôtel Hogon de Koro, I had a horrible headache and was instructed to use the rehydration packets CDC provided in my medical packet. Basically, these rehydration packets are, surprise, salt. So mixing them with water doesn't do anything to improve the taste of drinking liquid salt. Not one person at CDC warned me about this, but despite being upset about the awful taste of the rehydration packet, I was able to stave off the headache and the offending dehydration. I've since learned that it's much more palatable to fend off dehydration with Gatorade. Now I make sure to pack Gatorade powder when I travel to hot locales.

The accommodations that night were typical for this area of the world. The floors were concrete, and each room had an open window and a small window (think about the size of a chocolate bar) in the door that allowed a cross breeze to infiltrate the space, as there was no air conditioning. Electricity was available to keep the air in the room constantly moving, albeit with the assistance of an industrial-strength ceiling fan. The ceiling fan was so strong that I suspect it was used mainly to keep the malaria-carrying mosquitos trapped on the floor. That is, until about eleven o'clock when the generators for the compound were shut down. Once the electricity was cut, the oppressive heat stuck to you like a leech. It was expected that you would be in bed under a bed net to protect you from the mosquitos. The low temperature that night was around 90 degrees, and I found it difficult to sleep. I was very happy to have a shower right next to the bed in my room. So I exited the safety of my net-covered bed to take several cool showers throughout the night. Luckily, I was able to get a couple of hours of sleep and avoided contracting malaria and relapsing dehydration. The long trip back to Bamako the next day offered me the opportunity to catch up on sleep… The bumps didn't bother me on this return trip at all, as all I really needed was air conditioning.

As mentioned above, I wasn't able to secure a carved door or shutter as a memento of my visit to Pays Dogon. However, I was able to negotiate for a couple of masks that are symbolic of the area and the celebrations in which the Dogon people have participated for many decades. I purchased a small rabbit mask that was hand-carved and painted by artisans in the village. This was a gift for Savana. I decided I wanted something a bit larger for me to use as a focal piece in my home office. So I worked with our guide to see if the artists had anything somewhere between the size of the rabbit mask and a replica window shutter. After looking over several masks that didn't fit my indeterminable tastes, one of the artists went behind a building that housed hundreds of carved masks to retrieve something not yet displayed for visitors. I learned that artists artificially age their wares to give visitors the impression that the art was decades old (and therefore more valuable). I'd been warned not to attempt to buy anything that could be considered antiquity, as this would likely have been a breach of international law. So I was glad to hear that the mask now being presented to me was literally carved a few weeks prior, smeared with old motor oil, and buried with the hopes that tourists would see it when it was intended to be unearthed several months later and want it because it seemed to be much older than it really was.

Well, my inability to find anything in the already excavated inventory led them to give up and dig one up that was precisely what I was looking for. The mask, carved from a local tree, is raw wood without any adorning paint. This Kwele mask is that of a square-faced elder topped with two small full-bodied people meant to symbolize light and clarity (or good and evil). This particular mask hadn't *ripened* completely, so they explained the aging process to me, and I was able to get a pretty good deal. My lack of culture and fear of breaking the law worked very nicely in my favor this time around… not only did I get the mask for about a quarter of what they normally sell them for, but I also walked away with an education on speed-aging wood sculptures.

My return to the States after this trip involved a short three-day layover in Paris. As you've probably surmised, I am not a terribly sophisticated traveler. But like just about every other human on earth, I've been exposed to what the world has to offer outside the confines of the United States. Years of hearing stories, reading books, watching television programs, and seeing movies about locales across the globe have contributed to my desire to travel to see some of the iconic places around the world. Paris has always been one of the places to which I've been attracted, and I decided to experience the City of Light since the most expensive part of the trip had already been covered (another shout-out to the wonderful taxpayers of the United States). And luckily, I don't recall any television shows or movies that introduced me to the criminal elements in Paris to make me want to put my money in my shoes. After all, the movie *Taken* wouldn't come out for another seven years.

Tracey was able to fly to Paris the day before I was to arrive, and she had already checked into the hotel and made my arrival from West Africa much less stressful. After more than thirty years of hearing about Paris, I was finally able to spend a few days in this incredibly romantic and picturesque city with my wife. I was so overwhelmed with being there that I spent an inordinate amount of time-fighting back tears or actually crying tears of joy. I suspect I was driven to this emotional state by the fact we were fulfilling a long-held desire to see all the iconic architecture and visit as many museums as possible in a three-day stint. It was probably also the fact that I hadn't had my typical fare in two weeks and needed an injection of familiar comfort food. So after breakfast at the McDonald's around the corner from the La Familia Hotel in the Latin Quarter, I was able to collect myself as we headed out to see as much as possible. This was in the days before Fitbits, but we estimated our walking each day at about sixty miles. So maybe I cried so much because of the blisters that had developed on my heels and ankles.

What the Hell Am I Doing Here?

A year later, I was asked to return to Mali to check up on the computer program in the small HIV clinic and make any necessary updates. I was also invited to work closely with the National HIV Programme to develop a similar system, this time to collect data at the national level. I was excited to go back and catch up with the small HIV clinic staff (all three of them) and to expand my exposure to a broader array of colleagues, from the National HIV Director to the Malian Minister of Health. But if you're perceptive, you've already recognized my trips to Mali were separated by the terrorist attacks in New York City; Shanksville, Pennsylvania; and Washington, DC on September 11, 2001. While there was only a difference of a year between these visits, like the rest of the world, my balance had shifted from being open and trusting to being guarded and skeptical of others' motives. My first step off the plane onto the tarmac in Bamako was met with the realization that the world had changed. This time there were Malian military personnel all around carrying automatic weapons. I was also reminded that I was returning to the hottest place I had ever been in my life, as I think it was 95 degrees when I stepped off the plane and onto the tarmac at about 9:45 p.m. Immediately, I asked myself, "What the hell am I doing here?"

The next morning, my driver, Abdraman, from my previous visit, arrived early so I could make it to the National HIV Programme

Headquarters to meet with the Minister of Health. The trip through Bamako this time revealed something I hadn't noticed the year before on my first trip to Mali. A good number of cars on the roads had Osama bin Laden stickers emblazoned on their windows and bumpers. This was a stark reminder of how the world had changed since my last trip. I suspect it was mostly my heightened perception of the threat and not that these stickers had all of a sudden been delivered to the drivers in Mali like a new T-shirt to commemorate a recent NFL championship. These Osama bin Laden stickers were probably there the year before, but I was oblivious to them as I was captivated by the proliferation of 1980s Madonna stickers in February of 2001.

While security at the US Embassy was perceptively more heightened from the previous year, I found the people of Mali to be the same welcoming, warm, and loving folks I left the year before. There were more outward expressions of welcome from just about everyone with whom I came into contact this time around, making me feel protected more and more each day. I was principally interested in providing my service to the National HIV Programme and keeping as low a profile as possible until I could return to the States. However, the wonderful people I encountered worked hard to give me a great experience while I was there. I was invited to dinner at the home of a colleague from the National HIV Programme, where she introduced me to her brother. During this introduction, she mentioned I was from the USA. The two of them then began speaking very fast in a different dialect of cursive to which I was not accustomed (French), so I didn't know what was happening.

It turns out the brother happened to be the promotions director for the Senegalese National Soccer Club, and the 2002 Africa Cup of Nations Finals was set to happen during my time in the country. So I was invited to be a VIP guest at the next match the Senegalese club would be playing. Remembering back to how I likely offended my hosts when I turned down the goat head during Tabaski the year prior, I decided I couldn't offend another person with my selfishness. So on Saturday, January 26, 2002, I went to watch the Senegalese Club defeat Zambia 1-0 as a VIP. My status as VIP meant that one of no more than about ten resin chairs (among the concrete stands of a stadium with about thirty thousand other observers) was reserved for me. This was the most exciting sporting event I have ever witnessed firsthand. The crowd was loud the entire match, and they cheered at the amazing feats of athleticism regardless of the team benefiting. And afterward, the players from Senegal came to our area of the stadium to celebrate alongside us VIPs and all the other fans that were close by. It was a magical night, and I felt as if I was part of the collective Senegalese soccer family.

POTUS Comic Relief

In 2015, I was asked to travel to Kenya to fill in as the CDC Deputy Country Director for a couple of months. The timing was auspicious, as President Barack Obama was scheduled to visit Nairobi for his only visit to Kenya during his eight-year term. He was there to attend the Global Entrepreneurship Summit to spotlight the extraordinary potential of entrepreneurs in sub-Saharan Africa and beyond. In my duties as the acting CDC Deputy Country Director, I was principally responsible for working closely with the White House Medical Unit (WHMU) to assist in appropriately disposing of any medical waste generated by the WHMU as the result of the temporary field hospitals set up while the president was in the country. So I attended twice-weekly meetings with the ambassador and other senior-level attachés to assist in the coordination of efforts related to all aspects of the president's visit.

In one meeting, the ambassador explained that the White House Communications Office had asked for assistance with a speech the president was scheduled to give to the Kenyan people. Specifically, they were looking for a lighthearted opening line for the speech, as he didn't want this to be an overly stiff address. So the ambassador asked if anyone had any thoughts for an opening joke. After several seconds of awkward silence, I said, "Well, he could come out and say something about how nice it is to come home and spend a little time looking for his birth certificate." The folks around the table fell completely silent, as this was a semi-taboo subject in the diplomatic world.

Ambassador Godec sat there for a second and, with a half-chuckle, wrote it down to deliver it back to the WH Communications Office. Less than two weeks later, President Obama used a derivative of my joke in a nationally televised speech. I now have "Joke Provocateur for the President of the United States" on my resume.

CHAPTER 8

Glory Days

Everyone in my family, and anyone that's ever spent any amount of time with me, knows the apex of my sporting *career*. But nonfamily members don't know what drove me to that place.

Early Exposure to Team Sports

Football

My first experience with organized sports started in 1972 when Mom and Dad registered me to play football at Clairmont Park, just about five miles from our house on South Bamby Lane. I was seven years old and was *drafted* by the fifty-five-pound Packers. Back then, the focus was on weight more than age, as I think the intent was to provide some degree of safety to the players based on relative size rather than by age cohort. There's definitely some confounding between the two, but the first point of business in football was to prevent someone of my size (well below the fifty-five-pound maximum) from being hurt by someone my age but having about 20 percent more girth. Nonetheless, there were others on my team with about a year or more experience and in a much better place to understand the objective and rules of the game. So I was assigned the number 64 and placed on the offensive line.

I didn't really care for the game all that much, especially given I didn't have much control over what was happening. It also didn't help that in the first game or two, I was injured when another player's facemask somehow made its way to my nose between the top of my helmet and my facemask. I was so afraid it would happen again that my parents had an additional mask installed on my helmet. It was a *horseshoe* attachment that Larry Csonka from the Miami Dolphins wore in 1972 as well. I was the only one on the team with this attachment, so I started getting some attention, making my experience on the team a little better. That year our team, like the '72 Miami Dolphins, finished the season undefeated. Even though I wasn't terribly excited about playing on the offensive line that year, I learned that being undefeated had a way of making up for my disappointment in being a lineman. The stellar record that year came along with an invitation to play in the 1972 Turkey Bowl held Thanksgiving evening. I have three distinct memories of this particular game:

1. It was a cold and rainy night, making the conditions miserable. We got very muddy and were allowed to shower afterward in the facilities of the hosting school. I was (and still am) a very self-conscious person and didn't like the idea of being undressed in front of the entire team, unlike my teammate Rusty Laney, who was the first one undressed and in the shower and the last one out. So Dad helped me get cleaned up in the sink away from the other players.

2. Gale Sayers, who had just retired from the Chicago Bears, was at the game. Why? I have no idea. I have no memory of seeing him, but it was talked about for a long time afterward.

3. The game ended in a tie, and our season concluded without a loss. Close to how the Miami Dolphins did that year, except they actually won Super Bowl VII against the Washington football club and ended the year with all wins

(no ties). So yeah, I have a connection to the only NFL team with an undefeated season.

The second year of organized sports found me being a little more in control, as I was drafted by the sixty-five-pound Vikings as the quarterback. I suspect it was less about my stellar acuity and understanding of football strategy than it was about the fact I still weighed less than others, and being a lineman required you to not be knocked to the ground by a weak wind gust. This was during the time when Fran Tarkenton was the quarterback of the Minnesota Vikings, so I immediately wanted to have his number (10) to cement my reputation as a Hall of Fame-caliber quarterback (you know, people would automatically assume I was good just because I shared a number with Fran). However, the son of the head coach got dibs on this number despite his not being the quarterback, and I was assigned number 16. There's not too much in my memory bank about this season, except that I was in control for a large part of the game. This control fed my ego a good bit, and I really enjoyed the fact that people recognized me when I was off the field as the quarterback for the Vikings, albeit with a strange number. Nepotism can be cruel to an eight-year-old.

There were several more years of football in my youth, but just one garners memories to share here. The last year I played football was as the quarterback for the 1979 Duluth High School Wildcats B-Team. While we ended the season with an anemic record of one win, five losses, and one tie, I did have a few mostly fond memories of that year. I finished the year with three touchdown passes, one rushing touchdown, and one long kickoff return to the other team's seven-yard line. I also received the Best B-Team Back award and had my picture in the *Gwinnett Daily Newspaper*.

There is one additional memory I have of the season: During one game, I dropped back to pass, was blind-sided, and was sacked by the opposing team. I was hit so hard that when I got up, I went to the other team's huddle. I probably suffered a concussion on that play, but this wasn't a major concern back then. Dad used to call this "Getting your bell rung." We used to laugh about these things, but we didn't know how devastating these injuries could be until many years later. Perhaps this hit is what causes me to lose the ability to find words after about two o'clock every afternoon. Oh well, that hit is not what ended my participation in organized football…pride was the true culprit.

As mentioned before, I loved being the quarterback. Being the center of attention on the field suited my ego nicely. From my ascension to QB on the sixty-five-pound Vikings, I was the quarterback on nearly all my other subsequent teams. Looking back on my entire football career, I just realized that I never had a winning record as the quarterback. I wonder if my being a quarterback had anything to do with my team's lack of success. Nah, I'm sure it was mostly the fault of the coaches.

As I was about to advance to my junior year of high school, I had been practicing with the varsity team preparing for the spring varsity football game. The high school football coach announced to the entire team I would start the spring game since the varsity quarterback from the previous year was ineligible for the fall football season. So the intent was to give me some real-time game experience in advance of the all-important fall season. A few days before the spring game, the coach explained to the team that the previous starting quarterback would be starting after all. So, I decided that if he didn't want me to start the spring game, I wouldn't play in the fall. I gathered up my belongings after the announcement and left the fieldhouse, never to return. This was a huge decision made off the cuff, and I wish I had made a different decision. This resulted in me not continuing to play football, but you'll see later that this also had implications for my time on the baseball diamond.

Basketball

Soccer wasn't a very popular sport when I was growing up, at least not in our circles. Likewise, lacrosse hadn't broken into the American milieu in the 1970s. So in addition to football, we really only had two other options for team sports back then: baseball and basketball. I played basketball for one season when I was in middle school. I wasn't particularly attuned to the game and didn't find it appealing at all. The game was fine and all, but what turned me off were the uniforms. I hated tank tops and the short shorts used during this time.

I've mentioned before that I was (and am) self-conscious, and the 1970s basketball uniforms played to all my insecurities. In fact, sometimes in practice, we were subjected to separating into teams of *shirts and skins*. The thought of this still gives me the willies today, as with very few personal exceptions, I absolutely do not like to be without a shirt. So going to practice was always fraught with anxiety that I might be *drafted* onto the skins team. It didn't help my plight that I had serious deficiencies in this sport. Needless to say, I only lasted a single season, and I haven't feared having to remove my shirt to play a game to this day. I can say, though, that my lack of skill in basketball was balanced by my ability to foul other players with precision. I was always called for my fouls and often found myself being placed on the bench reasonably early in the game to prevent me from being tossed out of the game altogether. Oh well, it at least allowed me to put my warm-up jacket back on and shield my insecurities from the throngs of spectators (i.e., about a dozen parents) for the rest of the game.

Baseball

Baseball was my sport of choice from very early on. I started playing organized baseball about the same time I started football. The first team I played for was the Braves. I guess I was about seven years old, and I played first base. I don't have too many memories of playing baseball at that age, but I remember it was great to be on the field as a team *and* being alone when you're up to bat. Most of my early years in baseball were spent trying new positions and improving ever so slightly each time we played. One year, when I played for the Pirates, my coach wanted me to try out pitching. I went to his house a few times to practice throwing from a makeshift mound in his backyard. I was good enough in these practice sessions to give it a go in a game. Well, in my first pitching appearance, I proceeded to hit the first batter I faced square in the back. I settled down a bit and then hit this same player the next time he came up to bat. Besides being painful for the batter, it really took a toll on my confidence. So that was the end of my pitching career.

After several seasons trying different positions and finding only moderate success at the hot corner (third base), I moved behind the plate to become the catcher. This is where I felt most comfortable. Dad was my coach for several years, and he helped me gain an appreciation for the nuances of the game and how the catcher was really the one on the field calling all the shots. Remember my affection for being in control? While the pitcher is generally seen as the focus of the team when they're on the field, it is the catcher who's most in control (similar to the quarterback position in football). So Dad helped me develop a love for this position. As I'm writing this, I am just beginning to wonder if there was some subterfuge going on here. Catching is a grueling position, and it is tough to find people willing to take it on. So you generally have to give some type of incentive to folks to attract them into this position (like extra batting practice or soda, or deferral of registration fees). I don't know if I ever got any incentives for playing this position or if my parents didn't have to pay my registration fees. However, I came to love the position and all the good and bad things that came along with it. So if there was a stratagem at play here, it worked brilliantly!

One year after I graduated from Major League (about eleven or twelve years old), Dad coached both me and Robby on the same team. Robby was a left-handed pitcher, and I was the team's catcher. Dad used to joke that when Robby couldn't throw strikes, I would return the ball to him twice as hard as he was pitching it. Dad taught me how to play the ball and how to deke runners with fake throws. All this time I was getting better and really beginning to enjoy the strategy of baseball. I attribute my love of the game to Dad being so involved in each baseball season.

When I was twelve, the family moved from Atlanta to the small suburb of Duluth. After having spent several years building a reputation at Clairmont, I found myself having to try out for the league in Duluth. Dad was involved with the league but wasn't the head coach of a team. He ultimately assisted the team for which I was drafted.

So he told me to give it my all in the tryouts, and he would join the team as an assistant coach after all the drafts were made. During this particular tryout, I was asked to field a ball from the outfield and throw it to home plate. Well, I was so amped up that after making a clean play on the ball, I proceeded to throw the ball completely over the backstop behind home plate from deep in center field. I think the strength of the throw was more impressive than my accuracy, as I was drafted pretty high that year.

That year, I was fortunate enough to be placed on a team with several really good players, and the coach (Steve Evans) was quite good. I was selected for the All-Stars team two years in a row, and we won the district tournament and advanced to the State Playoffs in one of those years. During the years I played in Duluth, I began hitting really well and found myself in a battle against another player (Bruce West) to hit the most home runs throughout the season. I don't recall if Bruce or I hit the most home runs, but I know I hit the only moonshot that went over the lights! So in my mind, I was the winner.

Bruce was a left-handed pitcher and, even at twelve, had an impressive fastball and curveball. I didn't always get a hit against Bruce, but when I did, it usually went over the fence. He had great stuff, and I like to think he had the potential to make it professionally. Unfortunately, he fell in with the wrong crowd in high school and got into trouble. After high school, Bruce had a hard time adjusting to things and ultimately took his own life at the baseball park. I think about Bruce from time to time and wish we had stayed in touch after high school.

During the 1977 state playoffs in Ft. Oglethorpe, Georgia, I hit my one and only grand slam. Our team ended up winning the game 27-7, so the newspaper article only listed all the home runs our team hit that night (five). Unfortunately, the article listed my grand slam as a "four-run" home run. In addition to the glory of having my tremendous feat memorialized in the newspaper, I also received coupons for a free banana split at Baskin Robbins and one for a free dinner at Shoney's, both inscribed to "home run hitter, David Osborn."

My grandeur was dampened by these slights, but I am still quick to let people know I have a grand slam in my career statistics.

Dad was able to retrieve the grand slam ball and wrote all the details on it for posterity's sake. I still have that ball displayed on the table behind my desk. This is the most prized baseball-related possession I have, mostly because Dad inscribed all the specifics of the event on the ball. The writing is fading, but I can't bring myself to trace over his writing. This is another connection I still have with Dad all these years later that I just don't want to lose.

I briefly played baseball for Duluth High School and was one of two catchers. I played in the majority of games that year and had a mediocre season. The high school fences are much deeper than in the twelve- to thirteen-year-old major league fields, so I didn't hit any home runs. However, I was a decent defensive catcher and was allowed to play a good bit. I have just one real memory of my high school baseball career: I got a leadoff hit in a game that I was able to leg out as a triple. I slid into third before the throw made it to the third baseman. I bounced up, yelled "Time out" to the umpire, and proceeded to back off the bag to dust myself off. The third baseman tagged me, and I was called out. After contesting the call myself, Coach B. stepped in to take on the fight for me. It was to no avail, as the umpire was insistent that he had not called time out before I was tagged.

I broke a well-known axiom of baseball that says you should never make the first or third out at third base. I was crushed, but I also learned the lesson that the umpire is always right in baseball. And when you're the catcher, you're the closest player on the field to an umpire. The best way to influence them is to be affable so they give you the benefit of the doubt in close calls. So, I tend not to argue with the person with this type of power in most instances, hoping they give me the benefit of the doubt if I find myself in need of a break. There's no need to make someone dislike you and have a reason to rule against you somewhere down the line. Oh, and never leave the base until the umpire raises his hands and grants you time out.

Earlier, I mentioned my decision to quit the football team would impact my high school baseball career as well. At the end of my one and only high school baseball season, the head baseball coach handed out athletic letters and certificates to the players. I was surprised to find that I did not letter for the season. After all, several others with less playing time than I received letters while I only received a certificate. When I asked Coach B. about this, his reply was, "If we gave a letter to everyone, they wouldn't mean as much." It turns out the head football coach was also the high school athletic director I had quit on a few months earlier. I decided at that point my opportunities were limited under this regime and didn't sign up for the high school team again. Once again, I let pride get in the way of doing something I enjoyed. And similar to my experience at third base earlier that season, I found myself in a situation that could have had a better outcome had I only recognized the person with real authority as the athletic director and accepted his decision to start someone else in that spring football game.

Skipping forward about twelve years from my last high school baseball game to 1992, I found I had another chance to play baseball, if only for a day…

CHAPTER 9

Glory Days Part 2
My *Professional* Baseball Career

I don't feel my youthful sporting experiences constituted Bruce Springsteen-esque glory days, but I have been riding a glory train for the last thirty years tied to my one day with the boys of summer. As mentioned earlier, Tracey and I were married in August of 1990, and we moved to Fort Lauderdale, Florida two weeks later. I had just accepted a job with the Centers for Disease Control and my first assignment was as a public health associate at the Lauderhill STD Training Center. Shortly after arriving in South Florida, Major League Baseball announced that Miami and Denver were selected for new franchises in their respective cities. The Florida Marlins and Colorado Rockies would begin playing in the 1993 season. The addition of these two teams into MLB rekindled my interest in baseball and I decided I was going to do whatever I could to be part of the excitement surrounding this announcement.

I was a pretty competitive baseball player and I was still young enough to consider baseball as a career (or so I thought). So, I kept an eye out for how I could jettison my new career with CDC to play a child's game for a living. I like to embellish the story a bit so folks think I was a much better baseball player than reality would prove. Here's the real story: I was not invited to try out for the Marlins. The team announced an open tryout session to begin building their roster. The truth of the matter is it was more a publicity stunt than a true attempt to sign players to their roster. In fact, only one person was signed to the team that day (Ryan Whitman, a twenty-year-old right-handed pitcher from Palm Beach Gardens).

The tryout session was scheduled for Friday, February 28, 1992, at Bucky Dent Baseball School in Delray Beach, Florida. I had several months to prepare, so I began my own self-directed training program. Despite the fact that catchers aren't supposed to be fast (or really be in great shape), I began running around my apartment complex trying to build up my stamina and spent some time tossing the baseball with a fellow that lived in our apartment complex (Everett). Everett was always up for a game of catch after work. We weren't great friends, but we enjoyed throwing the ball and talking. We lost touch not long after the tryouts though. He knew I was going to try out for the team, so I suspect I laid low afterward so I didn't have to explain why I wasn't signed that day. I'm sure he thought I was a shoo-in given my ability to hit his target about 60 percent of the time I threw to him, and I didn't want to dash his hopes that he somehow parlayed all those hours of chasing my errant throws into being the friend of an MLB player.

The tryout was a big splash in the news, and I found myself in the background in a couple of news stories about the sporting spectacle. I still have some video evidence of my presence there that day. All the local news stations were there, as were the national news outlets (CNN, ESPN, ABC, CBS, and NBC). Sports Illustrated did a story about this in the following weeks as well. I was also visible in a photo on the front page of the *Sun Sentinel* newspaper the next morning—above the fold at that.

Being nervous about the tryout, I wasn't able to sleep very much the night before. And true to form, I left my apartment before sunrise that day and arrived at Bucky Dent Baseball School about two hours early. I was the first person to arrive, but it wasn't long before the crowd began pouring into the parking lot. As I recall, there were about six hundred wannabes there that day after all was said and done. Since I was the first person in the gates, I was allowed to sign in to get my tryout number. Pitchers were assigned numbers in the 100s, catchers in the 200s, and infielders in the 300s, etc. I was assigned number 201, the first available number for catchers.

This was my first time in any sort of park that had a professional feel. The Bucky Dent Baseball School in Delray Beach was established by (surprise) Bucky Dent and was laid out in the dimensions of Boston's Fenway Park, replete with a replica of the Green Monster in left field. Bucky Dent was a New York Yankee, so his interest in having Fenway Park as the footprint for his school may seem strange. However, he is widely remembered for hitting a three-run home run that gave the Yankees a 3–2 lead in the AL East division tiebreaker game against the Boston Red Sox in 1978 at, you guessed it, Fenway Park. Standing on a scale replica of Fenway Park with the Green Monster staring at you is pretty intimidating. I can only imagine how much more intimidating the real thing is. I'd like to say the park was what held me back from doing well during the tryout, but it was probably a complete lack of talent that undermined me that day.

Catchers were required to go through all the stations first, as we were then funneled to the bullpen section of the school to receive the pitchers for their specific attempts. So I was the first person of the entire group of six hundred participants to make it through all the stations for the day. I fantasize that someday the following answer/question will come up on *Jeopardy!*

Answer: The first person to ever try out for the Florida Marlins Baseball Club.

Question: Who is Darien Ogburn?

There's no doubt one of the contestants will get it right and disdainfully exclaim, "Of course, everyone knows this! Don't waste my time!"

Here's how the day went:

First Station: Timed fifty-yard dash. It's a shame we only had one attempt at this, as I'm sure I could have broken the fifteen-second mark the second time through.

Second Station: Catchers line up behind the plate, accept a pitch, and throw down to the second base. Your throws are timed from the clap of the ball in the mitt to the clap of the ball in the second baseman's glove. The coaches didn't tell us our times, but considering their laughter, I suspect they were excited to witness such cannons.

Third Station: Batting cages. Each player is given three pitches at three different speeds (eighty-eight, ninety-two, and ninety-four miles per hour). Understand that these pitches are offered by a machine with zero movement to the ball. So no curves, splitters, knuckleballs, etc.—just three flat lines. I hit all three eighty-eight-miles-per-hour pitches solidly. I hit all the ninety-two-miles-per-hour pitches pretty well also. However, the ninety-four-miles-per-hour pitches somehow mostly missed the fat part of my bat. I fouled two off and dribbled the last one back to the pitching machine. The whirring of the machines sounded a lot like a witch's cackle, but I got the last laugh when I walked out of the cage without being hit once. No physical bruises to show!

Other Stations: There were a couple of other stations set up for the infielders and outfielders. But since the real athletes had to go catch the pitchers, I wasn't able to do the easy stuff, like shag fly balls or take infield.

After having completed these stations, I was shuffled over to the bullpen section to prepare for the pitchers. I was instructed to don the catcher's gear and asked to wait for the pitchers to begin arriving at the mounds. I have four very distinct memories from this part of the tryouts:

1. Since the Marlins were just beginning, all the equipment was brand new. So, I had to remove the chest protector, shin guards, helmet, and face mask from the plastic they arrived in from the manufacturers. It was probably just from Sports Authority, but I like to think it was sent directly to the team from the companies that made them.

2. We had what seemed like an hour to wait for the pitchers to arrive, so I had a little time to talk with the coach who had lined up behind me to evaluate the pitchers and catchers. So I took advantage of the time we had to pull out a camera and ask one of the other players to snap a photo of me with the coach (who was wearing a brand-spanking-new Marlins uniform). The coach asked me why I wanted a picture with him. I explained I needed proof I was actually there that day. It was mostly to prove to Tracey that I was doing what I said I would be doing on that perfect sunny Friday in South Florida. Looking back on this now, I realize it turned into something much more than that, as I have used this picture as a conversation piece over the years to recount my glory days as one of the boys of summer (well, more like one of the six hundred other failed attempts to land that particular moniker).

3. Finally, the pitchers arrived and we received our instructions from the coach. Separate from the broad instructions given to everyone through a megaphone, as I crouched down and prepared to receive the first pitch the coach leaned over and whispered to me, "You're the catcher and have protection, I do not. I don't want to be the one stopping the ball since I'm not wearing the protective gear." I agreed and gave him my assurance that I would do everything I could to catch all the pitches.

4. They used radar guns to document the speed of the pitchers and the first fellow I caught that day topped out at ninety-two miles per hour. I don't think I had ever caught anyone with this type of velocity, so I wasn't accustomed to how to accept the ball in the mitt with a minimum of pain. So I basically caught seven pitches from this pitcher right in the middle of the mitt (and directly on top of my middle finger). While I didn't have to make any incredible saves to protect the coach, I did wince each time the ball hit my glove. About two hours later my middle finger had swollen to about twice its normal size and began to turn an

interesting shade of purple. Later that night my finger had turned almost completely black. And for the next three or four days, my finger was a mark of pride for me to share with anyone with the patience to listen to my brush with greatness.

About six or seven hours after the tryout began, we were ushered onto the field to hear the coaches take on the morning. There was a short speech about this being a historic day and one for which they were completely surprised by the turnout (obviously size, not quality), but the main reason for the meeting was to call out the numbers of the folks they wanted to further evaluate. The players called would then be divided into two teams for a short-simulated game on "Little Fenway." Cut to the chase here: they never called number 201, and I, along with about 530 other players, was excused for the day. I found this to be a blessing in disguise (no doubt assisted by cognitive dissonance), as I knew I could get back to our apartment in Plantation ahead of the big traffic and begin recounting my glory days and showing off my battle-tested middle finger before it healed.

While I wasn't able to fulfill my desire to be on the roster for the Florida Marlins as the team took the field on opening day 1993, I was in Joe Robbie Stadium on April 5 to watch Joe DiMaggio throw out the first pitch for the new franchise. And despite not having my talent behind the plate that day (the Marlins foolishly hired Benito Santiago in my stead), the Marlins came out victorious in a 6-3 win over the Los Angeles Dodgers.

Glory Days Part 3
Who's That in the Picture?

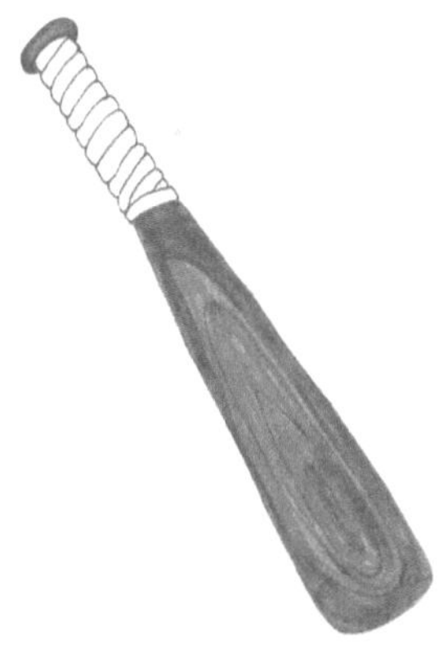

The stories I've told about my experience with the Florida Marlins have changed very little, as I never liked the idea of allowing them to grow to the point of complete lunacy. But there are lots of nuances about this experience that others may have taken slightly out of context, allowing me to passively bask in attention regarding my extraordinary baseball prowess. I've heard Dad tell people my experience with the tryout was more along the lines of an invited evaluation. And one time, when Nicholas was about eight or nine, I was surprised to hear he had mentioned to someone that I used to play for the Marlins. While technically correct, I was able to give a more accurate description of my experience without cutting off the conversation completely. It was a fortuitous incident in this realm that actually provided me with additional information I would use in future conversations.

Nicholas was invited to a friend's birthday party when he was eight or nine years old. This was one of those parties where we felt comfortable dropping him off and picking him up at the end of the party. Somehow, in the course of the day, Nicholas explained his understanding of my Marlins experience, which was then conveyed to one of the parents. When I arrived to pick up Nicholas, one of the fathers mentioned Nicholas' claim. A little clarification was given, and several of the other fathers joined in the conversation as we waited for the children to finish their birthday festivities.

Come to find out, one of the fathers was a Marlins fan and he asked a number of questions about my experience. The story of the coach instructing me not to miss any pitches came up, and the interested father asked if it was Fredi Gonzalez. I brushed this off because Fredi only became the Manager for the Marlins in 2007, and at the time, I had no idea that Fredi was in the Marlins organization well before that. This conversation led me to learn that the coach in my picture from that day was, in fact, Fredi Gonzalez. It turns out he had been hired by the Marlins before the tryouts to be the manager of the Single-A affiliate Erie Sailors.

I learned about my brush with Fredi Gonzalez about eighteen years after it occurred, in 2016, and now this is a focus in my "Glory Days" stories. He was the manager for the Atlanta Braves at the time, so I sent the picture and recounted the story to him in an accompanying letter. He signed the photo "You didn't miss it" and sent it back to me. I have this photo and the sticker I wore with my tryout number framed and displayed with many of my other baseball items. Second only to my grand slam baseball, this is a favorite possession of mine. Dad passed away in 2012, and I wish I could have told him about this connection before he died. It wouldn't have made Dad any more proud of me, but I'm sure it would have added to his embellishments of the story as well.

CHAPTER 11

Pivotal Moments

In my view, a quilt is a wonderful metaphor for life. Patches of experience, no matter how difficult, all contribute to the larger experience of life. Once you begin to understand that the experiences you have to underwrite your life, you will better accept both the good and bad as what makes your time on earth worthwhile. Everyone has challenges in life, and the last fifty-plus years have provided me with some. I don't want to say that mine are worse than anything others have experienced; they've just helped to provide additional threads to the fabric of my life.

You've heard about many positive things in earlier chapters, but I'd like to focus for a few pages on three challenging events that have had a significant impact on me over the years. As you might imagine, death will be the thread that binds these stories. Like most children, death wasn't something for which I had much experience early in my life. Of course, there were some distant relatives who had passed away when I was young, but I didn't experience the finality that accompanies death for those who lose the daily presence of a loved one. My first brush with death was a trivial experience when Robby and I received a BB gun for Christmas when I was about ten. After being given a number of *lessons* from Dad on how to use the BB gun (specifically not to point it at another person and how not to shoot your own eye out), I decided to solitarily venture into the wilds of our backyard to try my hand at marksmanship.

Early one morning, I quietly retrieved the BB gun from our pantry (it was stored there to reduce the potential of one of us accidentally shooting our eye out) and set out into the wilds of the turn-around to search for something to use as target practice. After a few shots at stationary objects (trees and trash cans, as I recall), I came across something a bit more challenging—a small bird perched on a low-lying branch that provided shade to our driveway. As I noise-lessly squatted and took aim at the tiny target about ten yards away, I thought to myself this would be a good chance to challenge my skill at hitting a semi-moving target. After all, it wasn't flying, but it was fluttering its wings a bit. I steadied myself, exhaled (as I was instructed in our *shooting classes* by Dad), and slowly squeezed the trigger. Much to my astonishment, it was a direct hit and the bird instantly fell to the ground. As I stood over the lifeless creature, the pride in my ability to actually strike the target was almost immediately replaced with fear and sorrow. My youthful exuberance tricked me into thinking the bird would shake off the shock of being shot and return to the air to avoid another embarrassing episode of a child netting him in front of his friends. I took a stick and prodded the creature a few times, encouraging it to get up and fly back to his family. Alas, it never did, and I was crushed knowing that I was responsible for taking its life. It was at this moment I began to appreciate the finality of death.

Wesley Alexander Edge

My sister Chris and her husband, Larry, were blessed to have three wonderful children: Cassie, Wesley, and Callie. All were born before Tracey and I were married, and we bonded with them in very special ways. I'm not exactly sure of the reason, but Cassie and Wesley would play "Tracey and Darien" when they were young. We loved these kids so much, and we would get together as often as we could before Tracey and I moved to Fort Lauderdale. Even after we moved, we would exchange *video mail* before the Internet (and FaceTime) came into the collective consciousness. Basically, we would use our video cameras to tape a letter to each other and send the VHS tape via the USPS. I still have these videos and bring them out on occasion to recall how silly the kids were when they would film themselves dancing to "U Can't Touch This" by MC Hammer.

Wesley was born with a congenital heart defect and had to undergo many surgeries throughout his short life. For reasons which I am still not clear, my connection to Wesley was extremely strong. Perhaps the fragility with which he entered the world contributed to the depth of the connection. His red hair and freckles endeared him to many people, but his presence was the tractor beam to everyone's heart. Wesley was a very creative old soul who seemed to live with the uncanny anticipation of a short physical manifestation on earth. Whatever the reasons, I was very close with Wesley.

Tracey and I moved back to the Atlanta area to be close to family again about nine months after Savana was born. When he was thirteen, Wesley was scheduled for another heart surgery at Children's Healthcare of Atlanta right as we moved back. The surgery was billed as an all-or-nothing attempt to get him into adulthood. The initial results of the surgery seemed to be successful, and Wesley was in ICU recovering as he dealt with several setbacks over the subsequent days. This was common after his surgeries, but he always pulled through, displaying his fighting nature. A day or two after this particular surgery, Wesley was losing blood, but the medical team couldn't figure out where the problem was emanating. The last time I went back to see Wesley, we spent a few minutes in superficial conversation before I realized he needed some rest. As I was leaving, he asked me to turn on the radio. My attempt to make him smile was to ask if he wanted to listen to heavy metal or rap music. His response was, "No, I want to listen to Christian music." That was the last time I talked with him, as he passed away the next morning.

Wesley's death was devastating to so many people, and I was no exception. I miss his creativity, smile, love, sense of humor, and red hair and freckles to this day. I have so many good memories of Wesley that there is no way his death will ever overshadow his life. My favorite memory is a story Chris recounts about when Wesley was about ten or eleven. Wesley was taking a bath, and Chris needed to retrieve something from the bathroom. Wesley, like me, was reserved and responded to Chris' knock on the door with, "Don't come in. I'm in the bathtub." Chris' suggestion that he cover his private parts with a washcloth was met with Wesley's reply, "Uh, I'm going to need something bigger than that."

Lauren Taylor Ogburn and Bebe Deanne Ogburn

As mentioned several times before, my sister Deanne came along when I was seven. Deanne was sort of an accidental child, but one who was welcomed into the family with all the awe and angst you would expect with a sibling group that now could seat an entire basketball team. Being the new addition to our family, Deanne was destined to be spoiled by everyone. I have lots of memories of Deanne when she was a child, but the good memories are difficult to recall because of the tragic life she endured and ultimately how it ended.

Deanne's first child, Lauren Taylor Ogburn, was born under stressful circumstances in the hospital and unfortunately acquired Serratia marcescens, leading to cerebral palsy. Deanne struggled mightily with taking care of a child with severe CP, and after some time, she met and married someone she thought would help bring her some joy despite the daily challenges she endured while caring for Taylor twenty-four hours a day. Deanne subsequently became pregnant and delivered a healthy baby boy, Dewayne, several years into her marriage, and things seemingly began to move in a more positive direction.

Taylor was a fragile child, and her brittle body ultimately succumbed to the burden of CP. She died on April 19, 2006, at eleven years of age. Deanne had demons of which many of us didn't know the extent, and Taylor's death led to a deeper struggle with all the remaining challenges in her life. These trials culminated in Deanne's untimely death on Tuesday, May 18, 2010, at the age of thirty-eight. While I am still convinced that her death was at the hand of another person, I have come to accept her death (and life) as something that was provided to all of those around her as a lesson from which to learn. Stay close to those you love, even when they don't want your help. Offer a way out of circumstances, even when you sense they're masking their struggle from those around them. And trust your instincts when you feel someone is preying on another person. Money is a strong attraction to many people, so it's best not to parade it in a way that attracts someone with ulterior motives.

My earlier comments about being able to find humor in most situations are challenged by the deaths of Wesley, Taylor, and Deanne. However, I have somehow learned to see the good in their lives despite the traumatic nature of their losses. In addition to Wesley's proclamation that a washcloth just wasn't sufficient to cover his nether regions, one story of Deanne brings a smile to my face every time I recount it. One afternoon, in a statement of teenaged braggadocio, I came home and exclaimed, "The breadwinner is home," to which Deanne responded, "Who won bread?" Bless her heart!

Defining Moment

Tracey and I had decided to wait five years after marriage before having children. We wanted to get to know each other well before introducing another person into our family. And almost right on schedule, Tracey became pregnant about five months after our fifth anniversary.

Combined with the withering heat of a typical North Carolina summer, Tracey and I were beginning to feel all the typical stresses that come along with impending parenthood. We had finished with the nursery and stocked up on all the supplies needed to care for a newborn, but we were still wondering if we would be good parents and how the introduction of another human being into our family would shift our daily lives. So like most young adults dealing with these things, we reached out to our parents to have them come to Greenville, North Carolina, to share in the birth of (and early days at home with) our firstborn. Looking back on this now, I realize that having both sets of parents there to help us through this experience was not just helpful but necessary for my continued existence on earth.

While Tracey was due to deliver at any time, the last appointment with her prenatal physician on Friday, August 30, indicated we couldn't wait for the baby to arrive on their own timetable. So it was decided we'd check into the hospital the evening of Labor Day (the irony doesn't escape me here) and prepare for an induced labor the next morning. Tracey and I alerted our families of the plan as soon as we confirmed everything with the physician and hospital, and so cascaded the parental plans of support.

Everyone arrived from the Atlanta area over the holiday weekend, and things began to hop around our tiny house on Mayfield Drive. This was to be the first grandchild for Tracey's parents and the seventh for my parents. So understandably, Tracey's parents were more involved in assisting, as this was old hat for my mother and father. I was accustomed to having a quiet house with just one other person around, so my stress level was beginning to rise, and I was happy to have some time alone with Tracey when we had to depart for the hospital on Monday afternoon.

As Tracey and I left our house to head to the hospital, the weather in Greenville, North Carolina, was partly cloudy with a slight chance of rain. We decided to stop by a fast-food restaurant on the way to the hospital to spend a few minutes together this one last time before everything in our lives would change. As we sat in Burger King snacking on some onion rings and french fries, it began to sprinkle. This slow rain continued as we checked into the hospital and didn't stop for another twenty-four hours. I don't remember the conversation as much as I remember the time we had together, just the two of us.

Tracey was diagnosed with type I diabetes when she was sixteen and began utilizing an insulin pump about a year before she became pregnant to better control her blood sugar levels during the stresses that typically come along with pregnancy. Knowing a bit about how diabetes can affect a fetus, we were all in on doing whatever we could to avoid any of the major complications. A couple of the complications we were particularly astute about were the potential for early delivery and having a baby that weighs too much. So when we found out Tracey was pregnant, we went in search of a practice that had experience with high-risk (most specifically diabetic) pregnancies. All in all, this was an uneventful pregnancy, and we had an above-average number of prenatal visits to assess the development of the baby to make sure that it stayed uneventful. As I mentioned above, the ultrasound in the final prenatal visit on August 30 tipped the scales for the doctor to decide we needed to deliver the baby about a week early. At thirty-nine weeks, the OB/GYN ultrasound technician estimated the baby to weigh about eight and a half pounds.

The first hour or two at the hospital were spent checking in, getting settled, and getting Tracey hooked up to a number of machines intended to track her progress and the health of the baby. Several times throughout the evening and during the night, the nursing staff seemed to be concerned with the monitors and how Tracey's contractions seemed to precede *decelerations* in the baby. We didn't know what this meant, but our own concerns began to increase as the hours went on. We were intent on delivering the baby as soon as possible so we could attend to these concerns directly rather than through the use of monitors. The staff began inducing labor in the early evening, and the decelerations intensified over the next several hours. Despite these ominous signs of fetal distress, Tracey was allowed to labor for nearly thirteen hours before the baby was finally delivered. As soon as the doctor arrived at the hospital the next morning, Tracey was prepped for an emergency cesarean section. I was allowed to stay while they got her ready but was then ushered to the waiting room to wait with our families.

I had never done any of this before, and I was sure that all the concerns of the last twelve hours would be over soon. I had complete faith in the process and knew that everything would be okay. After all, humans have been having babies for thousands and thousands of years, and for most of history, it has been done without the skillful oversight of incredibly educated and skilled medical professionals. Tracey's mother, on the other hand, had been through this several times and was visibly worried. I was content to calmly (relative term) wait with our parents in the waiting room until someone came to tell me that everything was over, and I could come back to see Tracey and our new child. Tracey's mother finally told me that it was taking too long, and I needed to forcefully go back to find out what was happening. I mustered up the courage and did what she suggested, and this is where my memory becomes extremely spotty…

I don't remember where I went or who I talked to, but it seemed to work because the next several minutes resulted in a complete shift in the trajectory of our lives. Here's what I do remember:

The doctor escorted me into the room where Tracey lay, and I immediately was concerned about the oxygen mask she was wearing. I was so troubled by this sight that I immediately asked (I think I yelled) why she had been intubated. They explained she had not been intubated but just needed some supplemental oxygen during the procedure, which was very common. However, the very next thing I heard the doctor say was, "You have a beautiful baby boy, but things don't look good." I replay this in my head every so often, and even this many years later I can remember the look on Tracey's face and how I suddenly felt like I weighed about a thousand pounds. I didn't collapse, but I couldn't move anything. My arms were heavy, and my feet were cemented to the laminate floor. All I could do was lean over and hug Tracey. She didn't hug back; her reaction was muted, and her stare was vacant. The only way I can explain Tracey at that point was stunned and quite literally in shock. I can only recount a few things that happened over the next several hours, as it was clear I was in shock as well. I do remember requesting to see our son and being told he was in the neonatal intensive care unit (NICU) on life-supporting machines.

When I went back to see him in the NICU, it was the first time I comprehended the situation fully, and physically seeing him with all the machines is something I will never forget. I marveled at how healthy he looked despite all the machines. Another thing that really stuck out was the fact that he was about three times the size of all the other babies in the NICU at the time. While the final ultrasound on Friday estimated his weight to be about eight and a half pounds, we were astounded that he had been born at twelve pounds five and a half ounces. His size definitely contributed to the decelerations

I mentioned earlier and ultimately why he had to be delivered via cesarean section.

We named our son Jon-Michael DeWitt Ogburn, a combination of Tracey's father (Alan Jon DeWitt) and my dad (George Michael). He was born at 8:39 a.m. on Tuesday, September 3, 1996. Several consults with pediatric/neonatal specialists happened over the coming hours, and after all the experts unanimously determined that Jon-Michael's prognosis was terminal, Tracey and I decided to allow him to advance to the next stage in his journey, as God had planned. Jon-Michael died at 3:40 p.m. on the day of his birth.

Nearly everything from this point on is a blur. I do, however, recall the absolute pride and the conflict of joy and pain when I held him for the first (and only) time. After the NICU team removed the machines, they swaddled him in a baby blanket and brought him to the room to spend his last moments in our arms. Tracey held him first, and she was so intent on looking at him with eyes that would never allow her to forget that moment.

When it was my turn, Tracey handed him to me so gently and with the instruction to hold him in such a way as to support his head steadily. I looked at him for what seemed like an hour, but I knew it was only for just a few minutes. I rubbed his cheek and forehead and marveled at how soft he was. Obviously, his eyes were closed the entire time, so I never had the chance to see them. Later, when I asked the NICU nurse about his eyes, she said they were a "beautiful blue/gray." There were a few times he moved in my arms, and despite my hopefulness this was a sign of recovery, I was told this was normal muscle movement as death approached. Luckily, Tracey's parents had the sagacity to take pictures of these happenings, and we now have some physical photos of this time to reflect on in addition to those in our memories. I can't bring myself to look at them very often, but I absolutely treasure them when I muster the courage to do so.

I mentioned earlier that rain began falling as we drove to the hospital that fateful day. It was almost as if God decided to cleanse the earth as Jon-Michael arrived. In fact, the soft rain continued nonstop the entire time Jon-Michael was alive. I think this was a celestial metaphor for keeping the physical environment pure while Jon-

Michael was alive. The rain tapered off shortly after he passed away. I love rain, as it reminds me of Jon-Michael's time with us. On the other side of things, I absolutely hate the smell of hospitals, as this reminds me of the struggle he had to endure.

I have no idea where this came from, but as I held Jon-Michael, I asked the hospital staff if he could be an organ donor. Ironically, a major contributor to his demise (his weight) was also the thing that made him eligible to be an organ donor. Jon-Michael donated his heart valves and pericardium, and in just seven hours and one minute on this earth, he was able to find and fulfill his purpose. We found out several months after his death that his donations were not able to be transplanted into others, as they tested positive for *Streptococcus D*. They were used for research purposes, and while they weren't transplanted in others, I am so proud of him for the lives he touched in such a short time. Tracey and I became ardent supporters of organ and tissue donation and have given speeches to encourage folks to consider this before they're faced with making a decision in the middle of a crisis situation. I still wear an organ and tissue donation support lapel pin every day and relish the opportunity to tell Jon-Michael's story when asked what the pin supports. The final point I make in my speeches is a request for people to be deliberate in their decision, regardless of whether they decide to be an organ donor or not. It is a tragedy for someone not to be able to donate not just because they didn't mark it on their driver's license, but more so because they never considered it.

The days that followed Jon-Michael's death were complete with nearly everyone in our immediate families traveling to North Carolina to support us. We wanted Jon-Michael to be buried in Georgia, so we had to wait for Tracey's uncle to get all the necessary documentation in place to transport him in a private automobile. This allowed us to receive a large number of family members into our tiny house to show them the nursery and photos as we reluctantly stepped into our grieving process. Everyone's trip to North Carolina was complicated by Hurricane Fran, which made landfall off the eastern coast of NC just two days after Jon-Michael's birth and death. In fact, I was so distraught after the events of September 3 that the doctor prescribed me Xanax to help me calm down and sleep. Well, I completely slept through Hurricane Fran as she ripped siding from our house. Tracey awakened me after the storm had passed to alert me that our house had sustained some damage from the storm. After asking what storm she was talking about, she and her father walked me outside to assess the situation. About three-fourths of the siding from the side of our house was missing. In a monotone voice, I told her to "get it fixed," and I returned to bed. When I finally woke up, I learned our neighbor, Reid Gaskins, had made all the repairs. While it was nice to have all the repairs taken care of while I was under the influence, I haven't taken Xanax since.

The person who was the most calming to me during the next few days was my eleven-year-old nephew Wesley (Chris and Larry's son). One morning I was sitting on the floor in the nursery looking at all the furniture and toys that would not be used. As I was trying to grapple with how to see the other side of these mountains of loss, Wesley came in and simply sat next to me. As he sat with me, he didn't say a word the entire time. Wesley and I always had a special relationship, and his presence that day was more helpful than all the counseling I've had since. As you're aware, Wesley died about a year and a half later, making those few minutes in the nursery with him all the more valuable to me.

Despite one of the opening salvos in this book indicating I bring humor into most situations, I find it hard to do that with Jon-Michael's death. I've had to come to grips with it over time, but it's been a decades-long battle. It's not humor, but I have learned what this experience has offered me besides pain—the ability to calmly accept challenges with which many other people tend to struggle. I've found that possibly the worst thing you could imagine ever happening is the unexpected loss of a child, and if you make it through that, you're likely going to survive not getting a promotion, missing out on a huge stock opportunity, not finding a Tickle Me Elmo doll for your child, or any other *misfortune* you might experience in this life. Tracey and I have had many people compliment us on our strength in handling this situation over the years. I don't necessarily see it as strength as much as I do survival. Basically, you have two choices when you're faced with challenges in life: You can either give up, or you can face the situation and keep moving forward…one minute at a time. Then one hour at a time, and finally one day at a time. We did it together, and we've been able to have a really great life so far. No doubt the arrivals of our daughter Savana and son Nicholas have added infinite joy to our experience.

When Tracey and I learned she was pregnant with Savana, all the fears came rushing back, so much so that it was nearly debilitating. It didn't consume us though. We took the lead on everything for which we had control to protect ourselves and the life that was now growing inside Tracey. We dictated to the physician's group handling this pregnancy how we were going to approach the pregnancy and the delivery plan. Luckily, we lived in a small town with a very connected medical community. In fact, when we went searching for a new prenatal practice to help us through this pregnancy, we learned all the practices in town had heard about our experience with Jon-Michael and they all wondered who we would come to if we decided to have other children. We selected a group that was 100 percent onboard with our desire to "tell them what to do." After all, the most ardent advocate for us was our personal experience. This new medical group wouldn't let us do anything unsafe (not that we would have), but they allowed us to be extraordinarily cautious as we progressed through the pregnancy. They also ran interference with the insurance carrier if we decided to do more than what was dictated in the policy, and in every instance, we were allowed to do more than the minimum even when it was not medically necessary.

With the assistance of this wonderful group of physicians, Savana was born in the same hospital in which her big brother died just thirteen months prior. Nicholas was conceived after we moved back to the Atlanta area, and while the physicians we chose to assist us in this pregnancy weren't privy to our specific experience, they listened to our story and gave us the same degree of freedom in developing the pregnancy and delivery plan as the group in Greenville that supported the pregnancy with Savana.

While I had tons of support navigating the first several years after Jon-Michael's death, I ultimately credit the arrival of Savana and Nicholas as my saving grace. I seriously question if I would have been able to survive if I didn't have these two incredible influences in my life.

CHAPTER 13

About That Title

As mentioned in the foreword, my family knows this story, but we never discuss it. From the stories in this book, the perceptive reader might conclude I have at least two potential targets for whom I would want to inflict bodily harm—people in my life that I feel have wronged me and/or my family in a way that I feel deserves a significant degree of retribution.

Let's start with the person I believe is responsible for Deanne's death. To avoid any sort of liability here, I must refrain from using their name. This person preyed on my sister and used her to access the money she received to take care of Taylor. I suspect this person never had any love or compassion in their heart for Deanne and therefore set a plan in motion from the time they met her to find a way to rob her of her bank account, even if it meant they had to take her life.

To exact revenge for Deanne's untimely death, I spent an inordinate amount of time and energy deciding how I could do so covertly to eliminate the potential for personal legal jeopardy. First, I didn't want to take the cowardly way out (like this person did themselves) by simply lacing their drink with a lethal concoction that would make them go to sleep never to wake. This was too humane to quench my thirst for retribution, as my intention was to inflict maximum pain and suffering and watch them succumb to the injuries that I myself introduced. So I came up with the plan to purchase an elaborate Ghillie suit and begin training to spend multiple nights undetected in the woods outside the person's abode. This would allow me to arrive well in advance to surveil potential witnesses and strike at a time when no one else was present. I didn't want witnesses around because my only target must be the person who directly perpetrated the crime against my sister. Even though those who helped this person cover up evidence of the crime bore some degree of responsibility, I didn't have the heart to cause them anything more than the emotional pain of killing the prime suspect. I would also need to improve my marksmanship from about fifty to seventy-five yards away from my target, as my last kill shot was from ten yards away when I shot the bird some forty years prior.

It is under the cover of darkness that I would slip into the woods just across the sleepy road from the house in which this person lived shortly after Deanne was buried—the house for which Deanne herself had purchased. I would take up short-term residence under cover of the undeveloped hillside beneath the thick brush to await the opportunity to provide the long-deserved punishment. The first strike would be debilitating but not immediately lethal. While they lay immobilized in pain, I would walk across the street and remove my camouflaged hat to reveal my identity. In my twisted view of just redemption, this approach would allow for maximum pain while giving myself the satisfaction of knowing they were fully aware of which indiscretion they were receiving capital punishment for. It all sounds very "Charles Bronsony" to me now, and until now, has remained deeply buried in the darkest recesses of my imagination.

Dad and I shared the belief that this person was wholly responsible for Deanne's death (our theory was that they deceptively and directly provided her with the ingredients that killed her). As my father's health was failing, he also began considering ways to take this person out, as he knew he wouldn't have to spend too much time in prison. In fact, he only lived about two years after Deanne's death. However, I'm happy to say that neither Dad nor I acted on our desires to take this person's life. The suspected perpetrator is alive to this day. Occasionally God allows us to witness his retribution, and he has done so in this case in a much more elegant fashion than lying in wait under the guise of darkness to exact my revenge. The person is now themselves in failing health, and while they're still alive at this writing, they certainly are not kicking.

Now on to my next potential target. After Jon-Michael died, I was in a very dark place. I was emotionally fragile and drastically needed something to help me see the world in a way that took me back to my generally positive mindset before the experience of losing a child. As you know, I grew up embracing humor in many instances, but I was struggling to find humor in anything. I felt like Tracey and I were victims of the medical staff we entrusted with the delivery of Jon-Michael. We were failed in a major way, and I found it very difficult to pull myself out of the rut of blaming myself and then blaming the medical team for the situation.

I did not have time to sufficiently grieve Jon-Michael's loss and really understand that his fate was more than a simple accident, as we learned that Tracey was pregnant with Savana just a few months after Jon-Michael was buried. So rather than planning some elaborate way to exact revenge on the person I felt was most responsible for Jon-Michael's death, I shifted my approach to resuscitate my sunnier disposition without taking another person's life. After all, I now had another child on the way, and I didn't want to find myself in jail for doing something that could easily be traced back to me. Therefore, I forgave the medical team for their inaction that ultimately resulted in Jon-Michael's death and have not allowed any lingering desire to exact anything other than legal remediation.

So who was it that I killed? Savana arrived in 1997, and I was still apprehensive about all aspects of life. Everything scared me, and I didn't know what to do. So I threw myself into learning all I could about being a good parent. I realized that I not only could provide Savana with a good childhood, but she would provide an exponential return on my investment. This would carry on when Nicholas came along as well, but this part of my story is related most specifically to my connection with Savana.

Savana and I have a very special relationship, and I have been fortunate enough to learn more from her than the reverse. I was astounded at how close we grew and the depth of the conversations we would have even when she was just two or three. I would hold her in my lap, and we would watch television together in the first four or five years of her life. I gravitated toward comedies like *Whose Line Is It Anyway?* which we called *The Funny Man Show*. We would laugh so hard together watching all these comedians improvise, and I consider these guys to be the genesis of my humorous connection to Savana.

We also used to watch *My Name Is Earl*. Tracey didn't approve of this brand of humor in front of impressionable children, so Savana and I would watch it when Tracey wasn't around. Unfortunately, Nicholas was always close by and overheard the program enough to pick up on a few of the unsavory/uncouth aspects of these shows. In fact, one day when Savana was about nine and Nicholas was four, they were playing in the garage when they got into some type of disagreement. Savana came into the house and said Nicholas called her a *dumbass*. And it wasn't long before Tracey recognized this was a line that Jaime Pressly's character from *My Name Is Earl* (Joy) used in many episodes. Well, that was the end of me being able to watch this program with the children around.

So over the years, Savana and I have strengthened our relationship by interjecting humor into all aspects of conversation. One day, completely out of the blue, and with no context at all, I told Savana, "I killed a man…but don't tell your mother." It had absolutely nothing to do with anything, but it instigated the intended reaction I was looking for…namely making Savana laugh. After a nervous and confused laugh, she looked at me and said, "*What?*" I've told this story many times to family members, but no one else finds it nearly as funny as I do, which is precisely why we don't talk about it anymore. Man, I crack myself up!

I guess the man I killed was actually the grudge-filled victim who found some sick satisfaction in planning to hurt people who aggrieved me and my family. Over the years, I have found the best revenge is to live your life accepting those things you cannot change and learning to love and cherish the people with whom you've chosen to surround yourself. I've had a great life, not despite these challenges, but because I've learned to live and thrive through them. After all is said and done, I'm delighted I found the strength to overpower the darker version of myself. While he's part of my life quilt, I'm glad I snuffed him out.

As part of the opening salvo of this book, I mentioned Dad's offer to answer any questions we needed the answer to before he passed. In addition to this offer, Dad implored his remaining children (Michele, Chris, Robby, and me) to "take care of your mother, and don't let her suffer." As I do in nearly every situation, I turned this incredibly poignant moment into a cheap chance to lighten the mood. I promised Dad that "we *won't* let her suffer. We will *make* her suffer." Despite my best efforts, Dad didn't laugh or even acknowledge my tone-deaf comment.

Almost a decade after his passing, Dad's appeal came into better focus for all of us. You see, Dad became Mom's primary caregiver and chauffeur as her mobility began to decline after she was diagnosed with multiple sclerosis in the 1980s. Exclusive of this ailment and a few other health scares, Mom benefitted from relatively good health for most of her life. So protecting Mom from some unknown menace (in addition to MS) was a far-off thought for us…that is, until the last few years.

Coinciding with the global pandemic of a novel strain of coronavirus in 2019, Mom began on a path of successive life-threatening accidents, requiring us (the children) to get more involved in making sure her needs were being met. The most life-altering situation came in mid-2021 as Mom was driving herself home from some innocent errand. A simple left turn across traffic on a major thoroughfare near her home resulted in her turning in front of another commuter approaching at about fifty miles an hour without sufficient time to avoid a collision. This began a series of incidents (mostly falls) that threatened her life.

The seriousness of Mom's condition and, learning from my ostrich approach to dealing with Dad's failing health, allowed me to become much more accepting that her time on earth was limited. Therefore, I began asking Mom questions about her upbringing and the trials and tribulations of her life. Between her recent health challenges, I did manage to ask her lots of questions with the intent to document as much as possible so she felt the love I had for her. I even had her teach me how to make her brand of potato salad.

As this book was in production, my mother passed away. I so looked forward to her being able to read this book and reminisce with me, and perhaps even revel in my recollections of the man she called her husband for more than 50 years. Having some suspicions that she might not make it to publication, I read her several chapters in her last few months. She laughed and cried as I recounted some of the stories. So, I was fortunate to get a glimpse of what her reaction would have been if she would have lived for just a few more months to read all the stories.

My efforts to learn more about my mother's past didn't get as far as I would have liked, but I take some comfort in recognizing her answers to the questions I did ask not only illuminated her past for me, but they seem to have benefited Mom in some ways as well.

The last several years have been difficult as we witnessed Mom's struggle to survive. However, since Dad's death we tried to help her live comfortably, maintain her dignity and what little autonomy she had left, and help her appreciate her surroundings. I like to think that we prevented her from suffering too much in her waning years. I don't know if our efforts met Dad's expectations, but we tried mightily.

I am very fortunate to have the last words Mom ever said to me etched in my memory forever. And I am happy to restate here the last words I said to her…I love you Mom!

Darien Ogburn is not an award-winning writer with a prolific library of works from which to peruse. He is, however, an eclectic consumer of life experiences with a fondness for storytelling. As a husband and father of three, he has experienced all the highs and lows one could hope for in a life closer to the end than the beginning. After having missed his opportunity for a professional baseball career, Darien set his sights on a three-decades-long profession in public health as a public health advisor and health scientist with the US Centers for Disease Control and Prevention.